basic
GERMAN
grammar

basic GERMAN grammar

John Clapham

JOHN MURRAY

Other titles in this series
Basic French Grammar Valerie Worth-Stylianou 0 7195 7121 9
Basic Spanish Grammar Richard Leathes 0 7195 7120 0
Basic Italian Grammar Tony Giovanazzi 0 7195 8501 5

© John Clapham 1996
First published 1996
by John Murray (Publishers) Ltd
50 Albemarle Street
London W1X 4BD

Copyright and copying

Layouts by D&J Hunter
Typeset by Florencetype Ltd, Stoodleigh, Devon
Printed and bound in Great Britain by the University Press, Cambridge

A CIP record for this book is available from the British Library.

ISBN 0 7195 7122 7

▼▼▼ CONTENTS

▼▼▼
INTRODUCTION

The aim of this book is to make the main points of German grammar accessible and memorable for anyone wishing to learn or revise them. It takes a very straightforward approach and does not assume that you are already familiar with grammatical terms.

- The purpose of each rule and structure is clearly explained.
- Examples taken from everyday language show how each point is applied and help you to remember the way it works.
- Activities give opportunities to practise or revise each point; answers to the activities are provided.

Basic German Grammar is suitable for independent revision or study, or for use alongside other course materials for reference and practice. It will be an invaluable help if you are in any of the following learning situations:

- working towards a language qualification or examination;
- taking a language component as part of a broader course such as Business Studies;
- brushing up on your German in preparation for a holiday or business trip to a German-speaking country;
- improving your grasp of German for use at work.

NOUNS
names of people, places and things

The first thing you will notice about German nouns is that they are written with a capital letter: das **A**uto, die **Z**wiebel. If you look up a German noun in a dictionary, you may find that it appears like this:

Stadt, n. f. (–, Städte)

It's a noun   It's feminine   It doesn't change   This is its plural
in the genitive case

These are the basic pieces of information you need to use the word correctly. 'Feminine', 'genitive' and 'plural' are explained below.

▼ Articles

An article is a word used in front of a noun to mean 'a' or 'the'. As in English, German distinguishes between the **definite** article ('the' = 'der/die/das') and the **indefinite** article ('a/an' = 'ein/eine/ein'): 'Gib' mir **das** Buch!' suggests a book the other person is holding, whereas we don't know which book is being referred to in 'Ich kaufe **ein** Buch'.

The tables below show you which article to use. This depends on the **gender** of a noun (whether it's masculine, feminine or neuter – see page 5 for more on gender), whether it's singular or plural, and on the part it plays in the sentence (its 'case' – see page 9).

▼ *The definite article*

	Masculine	Feminine	Neuter	Plural (for all genders)
Nominative	der	die	das	die
Accusative	den	die	das	die
Genitive	des	der	des	der
Dative	dem	der	dem	den

▼ *The indefinite article*

(Note that, as in English, there is no plural; the plural of **a** book is **books** and the plural of '**ein** Buch' is '**Bücher**'.)

	Masculine	Feminine	Neuter
Nominative	ein	eine	ein
Accusative	einen	eine	ein
Genitive	eines	einer	eines
Dative	einem	einer	einem

▼ *The negative article*

If you want to say 'not a . . .', 'not any . . .' or 'no . . .', you have to use **kein**:

Sie haben **keine** Zeitungen.   *They haven't got any newspapers.*
Er sagte **kein** Wort.   *He didn't say a word.*

	Masculine	Feminine	Neuter	Plural (for all genders)
Nominative	kein	keine	kein	keine
Accusative	keinen	keine	kein	keine
Genitive	keines	keiner	keines	keiner
Dative	keinem	keiner	keinem	keinen

▼ *The definite article and prepositions*

Sometimes – especially in spoken German – the preposition and the definite article become one word:

an das – ans	in dem – im
an dem – am	um das – ums
auf das – aufs	von dem – vom
bei dem – beim	zu dem – zum
in das – ins	zu der – zur

These are the most common examples.

▼ *Uses of the definite article*

The uses of the definite article in English and German mostly coincide. However, sometimes you need to include it in German where you would leave it out in English: 'Ich liebe **die** Natur' – 'I love nature'. Less often, German omits the article where it would be included in English: 'Es ist Mode geworden' – 'It's become **the** fashion'.

Unlike English, German includes the definite article as follows:

1. With **abstract** nouns:

   das Leben, die Freiheit   *life, freedom*

2. With parts of the body and clothing, if they belong to the subject of the sentence:

   Er steckte **die** Hand in **die** Tasche. *He put **his** hand in **his** pocket.*
   Ich wasche mir **das** Gesicht.   *I wash **my** face.*

3. With names of countries if they are feminine:

   die Schweiz   *Switzerland*
   die Türkei   *Turkey*

4. With days, months, seasons and meals when they come after a preposition:

   am Montag   *on Monday*
   im August   *in August*
   im Frühling   *in spring*
   nach **dem** Frühstück *after breakfast*

5. With proper nouns (e.g. names of people or countries) that come after an adjective:

   der kleine Peter   *little Peter*
   das heutige Deutschland   *present-day Germany*

   and in conversation:

   Hallo, ich bin **die** Anna. *Hello, I'm Anna.*

6. With names of streets:

   Meine Freunde haben eine Wohnung in **der** Sallstraße.
   My friends have a flat in Sallstraße.

7. In certain common phrases:

   Ich gehe **ins** Ausland.   *I'm going abroad.*
   Er wohnt **im** Ausland.   *He lives abroad.*
   in **der** Schule   *at school*
   in **der** Stadt   *in town*
   im Bett   *in bed*
   zum Beispiel   *for example*
   mit **der** Bahn (etc)   *by train (etc)*
   in **der** Nähe   *nearby*

▼ *Leaving out the indefinite article*

There are a few instances where English includes an indefinite article and German does not:

1. When talking about somebody's job:

Er ist Arzt.	He is a doctor.
Ich will Lehrerin werden.	I want to be a teacher.
but Er ist **ein** berühmter Arzt.	He's a famous doctor.

2. In certain phrases:

Er hat Fieber.	He's got a temperature.
Er hat Kopfschmerzen.	He's got a headache.
Wir haben Besuch.	We've got a visitor/visitors.
Ich habe Eile.	I'm in a hurry.
mit lauter Stimme	in a loud voice
Es ist schade.	It's a pity.
zu Ende kommen	to come to an end

▼ Activity 1 *Which article?*

Decide for each of the gaps in the following text whether you would use a) a definite article, b) an indefinite article, c) 'kein' or d) no article at all.

„Entschuldigen Sie, gibt's _____ (1) Bank hier in der Nähe?"

„Ja, in _____ (2) Königsstraße gibt's eine. Aber an _____ (3) Samstag haben _____ (4) Banken zu."

„Nein, wirklich? Aber ich habe _____ (5) Geld."

„Sie könnten zu _____ (6) Bahnhof gehen. Sie haben dort _____ (7) Wechselbüro. Woher kommen Sie?"

„Aus _____ (8) Vereinigten Staaten. Ich reise durch Europa."

„Sind Sie _____ (9) Student?"

„Ja. Sie auch?"

„Nein, ich bin _____ (10) Bankangestellter. Ich zeige Ihnen _____ (11) Weg. Ich habe Zeit. Heute ist für mich _____ (12) Arbeitstag!"

▼ Gender

In German, each noun has a gender – that is, it is either masculine, feminine or neuter. It is clear that **der Mann** should be masculine and that **die Frau** should be feminine, but **das Mädchen** (girl) is neuter, and **der Tisch** (table) is masculine, despite the fact that it's an object!

It is important that you learn each noun's gender as you learn the word itself, although the following lists may help in identifying the genders of new words.

▼ *Masculine*
- Days, months, seasons:

  der Montag, der September, der Frühling
- Many weather words:

  der Schnee, der Wind
- Many nouns ending in:

  -er: der Körper
  -ing: der Ring
  -ig: der Käfig
  -or: der Motor
  -us: der Kommunismus
  -ent: der Akzent
- Nouns made from verbs, without an ending:

  der Anblick (from 'blicken'), der Sprung (from 'springen')

▼ *Feminine*
- Nouns made from verbs, ending in -t:

  die Arbeit (from 'arbeiten'), die Tat (from 'tun')
- Most rivers:

  die Themse, die Donau
- Many trees and flowers:

  die Eiche, die Buche, die Rose, die Tulpe

• Many nouns ending in:

-ät: die Qualität
-a: die Firma
-e: die Reise
-ei: die Wäscherei
-heit: die Gesundheit
-ik: die Physik
-ion: die Nation
-keit: die Freundlichkeit
-schaft: die Gesellschaft
-ung: die Wohnung
-enz: die Intelligenz
-ie: die Industrie

▼ *Neuter*

• Continents and most cities and countries:

das heutige Europa, das alte Wien

• Nouns with the diminutive endings -chen and -lein:

das Mädchen, das Fräulein

• Nouns ending in -ma, -ment, -um and -nis:

das Thema, das Dokument, das Studium, das Ergebnis

• Nouns made from the infinitives of verbs:

das Rennen, das Singen

• Collective nouns beginning with ge-:

das Gemüse, das Geschirr

■ Words with more than one gender

Some words have different meanings depending on the gender. Examples are:

der Hut *hat*   die Hut *guard*
der Leiter *manager*   die Leiter *ladder*
der See *lake*   die See *sea*
der Tor *fool*   das Tor *goal, gate*

▼ **Activity 2**   *Work out the gender*

Put either 'der', 'die' or 'das' in each of the gaps.

1. _____ Arbeit ist interessant, aber schlecht bezahlt.
2. Siehst du _____ Häuschen auf dem Hügel?
3. Der Film geht um _____ heutige Deutschland.
4. _____ Regen war so heftig, daß ich zu Hause blieb.
5. Im Herbst ist _____ Landschaft am schönsten.
6. _____ Stadtzentrum soll sehr verschmutzt sein.
7. Ich habe _____ Übung ziemlich schwierig gefunden.
8. Ist _____ Winter im Deutschland immer so kalt?

▼ Making a noun plural

Like its gender, a noun's plural is best learnt when you learn the word itself. Plurals are often irregular (as is sometimes the case in English – children, geese and sheep, for example!). The main ways of forming the plural are as follows. Examples are given for each. Apart from the endings, the most important point to note is the umlaut which is often added to a, o and u.

▼ *Plurals with -e*
der Markt – die Märkte
die Wand – die Wände
der Tag – die Tage
der Ruf – die Rufe

▼ *Plurals without an ending*
der Apfel – die Äpfel
die Tochter – die Töchter
das Fenster – die Fenster

▼ *Plurals with -er*
der Wald – die Wälder
das Haus – die Häuser

▼ *Plurals with -(e)n*
das Hemd – die Hemden
die Hoffnung – die Hoffnungen
die Freundschaft – die Freundschaften

▼ *Plurals with -s*
(This group includes many foreign words.)
der Park – die Parks
das Hobby – die Hobbys

■ Plural only!
Some words only exist in the plural:

die Eltern   *parents* (die Mutter/der Vater)
die Ferien   *holidays* (one day's holiday = der Feiertag)
die Leute   *people* (one person = der Mensch/der Mann/die Frau)
die Möbel   *furniture* (one piece of furniture = das Möbelstück)

Other words **are used** mainly in the plural:

Die Nachrichten sind schlecht.   *The news is bad.*
Haben Sie **Informationen** über die Stadt?   *Have you got any information about the town?*

▼ Activity 3   *Plurals*

Put the nouns in brackets in the plural. You can use the examples above to help you, or look in a dictionary to find out the plural.

1. Hilf' deiner Mutter – sie hat alle [Hand] voll!
2. Wieviele [Cola] hast du bestellt?
3. Das Haus wurde in acht [Wohnung] geteilt.
4. Es gibt zuviele [Auto] und nicht genug [Fahrrad] auf den [Straße]!
5. Die [Bild] von Picasso mag ich nicht.
6. Wer hat dir die [Blume] geschenkt?
7. Der Geruch war so scheußlich, daß ich die [Fenster] aufmachen mußte.
8. Beide [Mannschaft] haben gut gespielt.

▼ Weak nouns

There is a certain group of nouns in German which take an -n or -en ending in every case except the nominative singular (see below for cases). An example is 'der Kunde':

Es stehen schon viele Kund**en** an der Kasse.
Kannst du bitte dem Kund**en** seine Quittung geben?

The group includes many common words, such as:

der Junge	*boy*
der Mensch	*human being*
der Franzose	*Frenchman*
der Kollege	*colleague*
der Kunde	*customer*
der Nachbar	*neighbour*
der Herr	*gentleman*
der Präsident	*president*
der Polizist	*policeman*

A few other nouns behave in exactly the same way, except that they also add 's' in the genitive singular. For example:

der Name – der erste Buchstabe des Nam**ens**
der Friede – es war eine Zeit des Fried**ens**

Others are: der Haufen (heap), der Glaube (belief), der Gedanke (thought). Das Herz (heart) also belongs to this group, but is 'das Herz' in the accusative singular too:

Das Kind malte ein rotes Herz.

▼ Cases

To understand how German works as a language, it's important to recognise the part played by each word in a sentence, whether this is in German or in English. Look at this sentence: '**I** gave the book to **him**'. Here we use two different 'cases' to make a clear grammatical distinction between the two people involved: the one who gives the book and the one to whom it is given.

There are four cases in German: nominative, accusative, genitive and dative. We use these in English too, but because the **form** of the word rarely changes, we don't usually notice.

In German the article changes (e.g. **das** Buch becomes **dem** Buch) according to which case the noun is in. Pronouns (e.g. ich, du) change too.

Let's look at the function of the four cases, firstly by studying some English examples. In the sentence below there is an example of each of the four cases in English.

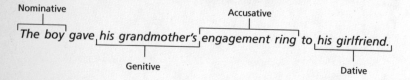

▼ *Nominative*

'The boy' is the **subject** of the sentence, the person who carries out the action. The noun 'boy' is therefore in the nominative case. If you wanted to add another noun to 'complement' or give more information to the first – e.g. 'The boy who is a footballer' – 'footballer' would be nominative too.

▼ *Accusative*

'The engagement ring' is the **direct object** of the sentence – the person or thing that has something done to it. The ring **is given**. It is therefore in the accusative case.

▼ *Genitive*

The genitive case is to do with **belonging** (i.e. 'of'). In our sentence the engagement ring belonged to the boy's grandmother, so 'grandmother' is in the genitive.

▼ *Dative*

Someone **to whom** you give, show or write something is the **indirect object**. To whom does the boy give the ring? To his girlfriend, so she's the indirect object and in the dative. (Quick check: if you give a friend a birthday present, which is the direct and which the indirect object? Don't always rely on finding the word 'to' in English!)

To summarise:

The nominative is used (a) for the subject and (b) for the complement.

The accusative is used for the direct object.

The genitive is used to show belonging (possession) – to translate 'of'.

The dative is used for the indirect object.

▼ Activity 4   *Which case?*

Can you work out which cases the underlined words are in?

Jack and <u>his mother</u> (1) lived in a small flat on the edge of <u>the council estate</u> (2). <u>They</u> (3) were very poor. One day Jack's mother gave <u>him</u> (4) <u>some money</u> (5) to buy bread and a tin of soup at the supermarket. She could only spare <u>a couple of pounds</u> (6) because they needed <u>the rest</u> (7) to pay <u>the bills</u> (8). But Jack was <u>a lazy boy</u> (9). On the way to the supermarket he passed the <u>newsagent's</u> (10) shop which also sold <u>bread and tinned food</u> (11). While he was there, the newsagent offered <u>Jack</u> (12) <u>a lottery ticket</u> (13), so he took <u>that</u> (14) instead, and then bought <u>a bar of chocolate</u> (15) with the change. He went home and gave <u>the lottery ticket</u> (16) to <u>his mother</u> (17). 'You mean you've spent <u>this week's</u> (18) <u>money</u> (19) on a lottery ticket!' she cried. 'Give <u>it</u> (20) to <u>me</u> (21)! Which <u>numbers</u> (22) have we got?'

Let's look at some examples of the cases in German.

▼ *Nominative*
is used for . . .

(a) the subject:

Der Junge kauft einen Hamburger.

(b) the complement:

Seine Mutter ist **eine berühmte Politikerin.**

▼ *Accusative*
is used for . . .
the direct object:

Der Junge kauft **einen Hamburger.**

'Es gibt' ('there is/there are') also takes the accusative:

Es gibt Kekse und **einen** Apfel.

It's important to remember that the object can come first in a German sentence: 'Den Käse hat Peter gegessen' does not mean that the cheese ate Peter!

▼ *Genitive*
is used for . . .
possession:

Die Tür **des Zimmers** ist zu.

In the genitive singular, masculine and neuter nouns add -s or (if the word ends in s, z, ß or has only one syllable) -es:

Die Farbe **des Autos** habe ich vergessen.
Ich habe den Computer **meines Sohnes** ausgeliehen.

Possession can also be expressed by adding an -s, as in English, but without the apostrophe: Peters Auto.

▼ *Dative*
is used for . . .
the indirect object:

Er schreibt **seiner Freundin** einen Brief.

In the dative plural nouns must end in n, unless they form their plural with s:

Er hat zwei **Kinder.**
Er gibt **den Kindern** ihr Taschengeld.

▼ *Cases in time expressions*

The **accusative** in German is often used to show

(a) how long something lasts:

Sie arbeitet **eine Stunde.**

(b) exactly when something happens:

Letzten Samstag gingen wir ins Kino.

The **genitive** is used when the time something happened is vague:

Eines Tages verschwand die Katze.

or to describe something which happens regularly:

Sonntags spiele ich Tennis. *(= every week)*

▼ Activity 5 *Use the correct case*

a) **Decide which case each noun in brackets should be in.**
b) **Make any necessary changes to the noun and its article.**

Claudia!
Komme später. Ich bringe [der Hund] zum Tierarzt. Er hat [ein Knochen] hinuntergeschluckt! Mach' bitte [die Kinder] [ein Wurstbrot] – es gibt [eine Gurke] im Kühlschrank und [ein Brot] findest du auf dem Regal. Ruf' bitte [der Vater] an – ich habe [das Auto] [sein Kollege] ausgeliehen. Ich vergesse immer [sein Name]. Wenn du [der Nachbar] siehst, sag' ihm ich hole [die Fotos] [seine Frau] an [der Montag]. Habe heute [keine Zeit]!
Mama

▼▼▼
ADJECTIVES
describing people, places and things

Adjectives are words which tell us more about nouns or pronouns: a **green** apple, an **Italian** car, an **unexpected** present, she's **tired**. How many English adjectives can you think of to complete this phrase: 'a . . . meal'? Being able to use a range of adjectives correctly in German will add a great deal more interest to what you're saying.

▼ Activity 1   *Spot the adjective*

Underline the adjectives in the following text. There are eight of them!

Der neue Roman von Waltraud Anna Mitgutsch . . .
. . .ist die Geschichte einer jungen Frau, deren Kind autistisch ist. Das Buch ist erschütternd und oft traurig. Es ist aber auch eine tolle Liebesgeschichte zwischen Mutter und Kind. Die österreichische Schriftstellerin hat schon wieder eine spannende Erzählung geschrieben.

Did you notice that some of the adjectives in the text came before the noun and that others came after it? If a German adjective comes **in front of** the noun, it has to agree with it, that is take an ending: 'der Roman ist **neu**' but 'der **neue** Roman'.

▼ Making adjectives agree

The endings on adjectives vary according to the noun's gender and case (see pages 5 and 9), but they also depend on **which article** is used: '**ein neuer** Roman' but '**der neue** Roman'.

We can divide the endings into groups according to which article comes in front of the adjective. There are two main groups: the **der** group and the **ein** group. The **der** group endings are also used after demonstrative adjectives (see page 18).

Let's list these groups of endings. Although they may look daunting at first, you'll soon discover that, in the majority of cases, the ending you need is -e or -en.

- The **der** group (also used after dieser, jeder, jener, mancher, welcher and solcher; see page 18).

	Masculine	Feminine	Neuter	Plural
Nominative	E	E	E	EN
Accusative	EN	E	E	EN
Genitive	EN	EN	EN	EN
Dative	EN	EN	EN	EN

Some examples:

Nom. Der dunkelhaarige Junge ist mein Neffe, und das kleine Mädchen ist die jüngste Tochter meines Bruders.
Acc. Nein, bring' den schwarzen Mantel, nicht die alte Jacke! Das grüne Hemd trägst du auch nie.
Gen. Liest du wirklich eine Geschichte der russischen Revolution?
Dat. Ich habe es irgendwo in der heutigen Zeitung gelesen.

- The **ein** group (Remember there is no plural of the word ein.)

	Masculine	Feminine	Neuter	Plural
Nominative	ER	E	ES	E
Accusative	EN	E	ES	E
Genitive	EN	EN	EN	ER
Dative	EN	EN	EN	EN

Some examples:

Nom. Ein goldener Strand, ein blaues Meer, freundliche Leute . . . was erwartet man noch vom Urlaub?
Acc. Wir haben eine gute Suppe gegessen, und dann noch ein riesiges Schnitzel.
Gen. Hast du die Telefonnummer eines billigen Hotels?
Dat. Den Tee findest du in einer kleinen Dose.

The endings after **kein** (no) and the possessive adjectives (**mein, dein, sein**, etc. – see page 22) are the same as those of the **ein** group, **except** in the nominative, accusative and genitive plural where the ending is -en.

Examples:

Keine interessanten Leute sind gekommen.
Darf ich deine roten Schuhe ausleihen?

■ **Some adjectives that change**

Some adjectives change when you add endings. Watch out for the following:

dunkel – eine **dunkle** Nacht
teuer – ein **teures** Geschenk
hoch – ein **hohes** Haus

▼ **Activity 2** *Making the adjectives agree*

Decide whether the adjectives in brackets should agree with the noun they describe. Add an ending if necessary.

„Sabine! Wie war dein Urlaub in Schottland?"
„Ach, wir haben [wunderschön] Tage dort verbracht. Wir haben in einem [klein] Häuschen gewohnt. Von einem Fenster konnte man [hoch] Berge sehen, und vom anderen das [blau] Meer."
„Wirklich? Und wie hast du das [schottisch] Essen gefunden?"
„Gut. Ich bin ziemlich [dick] geworden wegen der [gut] Kekse. Nur der Haggis hat mir nicht geschmeckt – das ist ein [seltsam] Gericht."
„Und wie waren die Leute?"
„Sehr [freundlich]. In einem [naheliegend] Dorf gab es ein [gemütlich] Lokal, und dort haben wir uns mit [interessant] Leuten unterhalten."

▼ *Other adjective endings*

There are some other groups of endings which are used as follows:

1. When there is **no word** in front of the adjective. These are known as **strong** endings.

	Masculine	Feminine	Neuter	Plural
Nominative	ER	E	ES	E
Accusative	EN	E	ES	E
Genitive	EN	ER	EN	ER
Dative	EM	ER	EM	EN

For example:

Bei regnerisch**em** Wetter
Nach viel**en** Tagen sonnig**en** Wetters

2. After **einige, wenige, ein paar, manche** (in the plural), **viele** and **mehrere**:

	Plural
Nominative	E
Accusative	E
Genitive	ER
Dative	EN

For example:

Ein paar reiche Leute
Viele große Häuser

3. After **alle**
The demonstrative adjective (see page 18) and the possessive adjective (see page 22) take the same ending as alle. Any other adjective takes -en.

Nominative	alle diese (meine) neuen Bücher
Accusative	alle diese (meine) neuen Bücher
Genitive	aller dieser (meiner) neuen Bücher
Dative	allen diesen (meinen) neuen Büchern

4. After **nichts** etc.
After etwas, viel, soviel, wenig, nichts and allerlei the adjective (a) has a capital letter: etwas **N**eues, nichts **I**nteressantes (but ander, möglich, übrig and einzig keep the small letter: Ich habe nichts anderes erwartet). (b) takes the following endings:

Nominative	ES
Accusative	ES
Genitive	EN
Dative	EM

■ **How to say 'with best wishes'**
Note the phrases **Alles Gute** ('all the best') and **Alles Liebe** ('lots of love'), which you might use to end a letter to a friend. The adjective after **alles** only takes an -e.

5. Derselbe (the same)

The first part declines like the definite article and the second half like an adjective after the definite article:

	Masculine	Feminine	Neuter	Plural
Nominative	derselbe	dieselbe	dasselbe	dieselben
Accusative	denselben	dieselbe	dasselbe	dieselben
Genitive	desselben	derselben	desselben	derselben
Dative	demselben	derselben	demselben	denselben

▼ Activity 3   *Other adjective endings*

Add the correct endings to the adjectives in these sentences.

1. Es gibt wenige gut____ Programme im Fernsehen.
2. Wer ist der Mann mit schwarz____ Haaren?
3. Wir waren in [derselbe] _____ Schule.
4. Ich möchte etwas Süß____ essen.
5. Ich kenne die Eltern all____ dies____ Kinder.

▼ This and that – demonstrative adjectives

The most important of these are dieser and jener, 'this' and 'that'. 'Jener' is only used when you want to contrast two things; when pointing at or showing things, Germans are more likely to use 'dieser'. These words are made up of two parts: a stem and an ending.

The stems

dies-	this	manch-	many a, many
jed-	each, every	solch-	such
jen-	that	welch-	which

The endings

	Masculine	Feminine	Neuter	Plural
Nominative	ER	E	ES	E
Accusative	EN	E	ES	E
Genitive	ES	ER	ES	ER
Dative	EM	ER	EM	EN

Some examples:

Dieser Film ist sehr spannend.
Diese Frau meine ich nicht, sondern jene mit dem großen Hund.
Ich habe jedes Wort gehört!
Solche Leute trifft man selten.

▼ Activity 4   *Dieser*

Fill in the gaps in this conversation with the correct form of dieser.

„Warum darf ich nicht mit _____ (1) Zug fahren?"
„Weil _____ (2) Fahrkarte nicht gültig ist! Gehen Sie zum Informationsschalter . . ."
„Zum welchem?"
„In _____ (3) Bahnhof gibt's nur einen! Gehen Sie in _____ (4) Richtung. Dort zahlen Sie einen Zuschlag."
„Okay."
„_____ (5) Studenten gehen mir auf die Nerven!"

▼ Making comparisons

If we compare one thing with another in English, we add -er or -est to the adjective: this house is nicer than ours (the comparative), this house must be the nicest in the street (the superlative). This is more or less what you do in German:

Dieses Haus ist schöner als unseres.
Dieses Haus muß das schönste in der Straße sein/ Dieses Haus ist am schönsten.

Unlike in English, where longer adjectives are compared with 'more' or 'most', German **never** uses mehr or meist. '**More** interesting' is 'interessanter'. The only exception is when a past participle is used:

Das **am meisten verwendete**   *The most used washing powder*
Waschmittel

If the adjective only has one syllable and the vowel is a, o or u, you usually add an umlaut:

groß, größer, am größten (also note it has no added s)
alt, älter, am ältesten
lang, länger, am längsten

There is no umlaut in the comparative and superlative forms of bunt, dunkel, voll or klar, to name the commonest exceptions to this rule!

The superlative form ends in -esten if it makes the word easier to say; usually in adjectives ending in d, t, s, sch or z:

am bunt**esten**, am kürz**esten**.

▼ Activity 5 *Comparative and superlative forms*

Can you make the comparatives and superlatives of the following adjectives?

1. kalt –   am –
2. schnell –   am –
3. dunkel –   am –
4. hart –   am –

▼ *Endings*

Like other adjectives, comparatives and superlatives need endings if they come in front of the noun:

ein schneller**er** Zug
der schnell**ste** Zug

▼ *Irregular adjectives*

We have these in English too. Think about 'good, better, best' and 'bad, worse, worst'.

The main ones in German are:

hoch, **höher** (no c), höchst
nah, näher, **nächst**
gut, **besser, best**
viel, **mehr**, meist

▼ Than and as

When we make comparisons in English we use the words 'than' and 'as'. German uses als and wie:

More expensive than: Dieser Mantel ist teurer als der schwarze.
Not as expensive as: Der schwarze Mantel ist nicht so teuer wie der andere.
Less expensive than: Der schwarze Mantel ist weniger teuer als der andere.
(Just) as expensive as: Der schwarze Mantel ist (eben) so teuer wie der andere.

▼ Activity 6   *Making comparisons*

Translate the words in brackets in the advertisement. Remember to put the right endings on the adjectives where necessary.

ZISCH – wahrscheinlich [the best] Abspülmittel der Welt!
Unser Produkt ist vielleicht [more expensive than] andere, hat [a more stupid] Namen, und ist nur in [the most exclusive] Geschäften zu kaufen. Zisch ist aber [as clear as] Wasser, und hat [a better smell than] frische Blumen. Mit Zisch ist das Abwaschen [less boring] – und Ihre Nachbarn werden sich über [the cleanest] Teller in der Straße wundern.

▼ Adjectives from place names

To say, for example, 'the London Underground' or 'Cologne cathedral':
(a) you keep the capital letter
(b) you just put -er on the place name and it never changes.
So we have:

die Londoner U-Bahn
der Kölner Dom.

▼ Adjectives used as nouns

Many adjectives can be made into nouns in German, simply by giving them a capital letter: 'der Alte' is the old man, 'die Deutsche' is the German woman. Their endings change just as if they were still adjectives, e.g. Ich sehe den Alten.

Other common ones (these are only the masculine forms) are:

der Bekannte	*the acquaintance*
der Erwachsene	*the grown up, adult*
der Fremde	*the stranger, foreigner*
der Verwandte	*the relative*
der Reisende	*the traveller*

▼ Activity 7 *Making adjectives into nouns*

Make the following adjectives into nouns, making sure that you add the correct case endings.

1. Wir besuchten unsere [verwandt] ____ in Berlin.
2. Ich begegnete einem [bekannt] ____ in der Stadt.
3. Sie ist die Tochter einer [deutsch] ____.
4. Er sieht wie ein [fremd] ____ aus.

▼ Mein, dein, sein, etc (= my, your, his, etc) – possessive adjectives

Below are the possessive adjectives in German – that is, the words you use to say to whom something belongs.

Ich *(I)* mein *(my)*
du *(you)* dein *(your)*
er *(he)* sein *(his)*
sie *(she)* ihr *(her)*
es *(it)* sein *(its)*
Sie *(you)* Ihr *(your)*

wir *(we)* unser *(our)*
ihr *(you)* euer *(your)*
sie *(they)* ihr *(their)*
Sie *(you)* Ihr *(your)*

Because these words are adjectives, they take endings depending on the noun they go in front of. For example:

Meine Mutter
Die Brille meines Vaters
Hast du meinen Regenschirm gesehen?

These are the endings they take:

	Masculine	Feminine	Neuter	Plural
Nominative	–	E	–	E
Accusative	EN	E	–	E
Genitive	ES	ER	ES	ER
Dative	EM	ER	EM	EN

Note that:

1. when 'euer' has an ending, it drops the second -e: 'eure Mutter'.
2. the possessive adjective of Sie has a capital too: 'Wie geht's Ihrer Schwester?'

■ What to do in letters

In letters, the familiar forms 'Du' and 'Ihr' and the possessive adjectives 'Dein' and 'Euer' are written with capitals.

▼ Activity 8   *Possessive adjectives*

Put the possessive adjectives in the correct form in the letter below.

Liebe Gabi!
Vielen Dank für [your] Brief. Ich freue mich zu hören, daß es [your] Mutter jetzt besser geht. Hat sie [her] altes Auto noch? Vielleicht können wir es für [our] Urlaub ausleihen? Ich habe schon ein Zelt von [my] Bruder. Er ist schon aus Südamerika zurück, und erzählt von [his] Abenteuern! Ich hoffe auch, den Campingherd [of my] Eltern mitnehmen zu können . . .
Alles Liebe
Birgit.

▼▼▼
ADVERBS
describing when, where and how something is done

Adverbs are so called because they usually **add** information to the verb. In English many adverbs end in -ly but there are also some irregular ones:

He ran quick**ly**.
I can't cook very **well**.

Adverbs can also describe an adjective or another adverb:

That's **extremely** unlikely.
She spoke **very** sadly.

▼ *When?*
• An adverb can tell us **when** an action takes place:

Ich habe ihn **gestern** getroffen.	I met him **yesterday**.
Wir fahren **im Sommer** nach Deutschland.	We're going to Germany **in the summer**.
Du sollst ihn **sofort** anrufen!	You should ring him **straight away**!

There is a range of adverbs to describe **how often** something happens:

immer	oft	manchmal	selten	nie
always	*often*	*sometimes*	*seldom*	*never*

▼ *How?*
• You can use an adverb or adverbial phrase to say **how** an action takes place:

Er arbeitet **langsam**.	He works **slowly**.
Ich esse **gern** Knödel.	I like eating dumplings (literally: I eat dumplings **willingly**).
Fährst du immer **mit dem Auto**?	Do you always go **by car**?

▼ *Where?*

• Adverbs describe **where** an action takes place:

Kann man **dort** Briefmarken kaufen?

*Can you buy stamps **there**?*

Ich habe meinen Regenschirm **irgendwo** vergessen.

*I've left my umbrella **somewhere**.*

▼ Forming adverbs

In most cases in German you can simply use the adjective:

Sie singt **schön**.

She sings beautifully.

Du fährst zu **schnell**.

You drive too fast.

However, there are some common adverbs with the endings -lich, -s, -weise and -lang. Here are some of them:

sicherlich	*certainly*
morgens, abends (etc)	*in the morning, evening (etc)*
links/rechts	*on the left/right*
besonders	*particularly*
normalerweise	*normally*
glücklicherweise	*fortunately*
teilweise	*partly*
stundenlang, tagelang (etc)	*for hours, days (etc)*

▼ Activity 1   *Forming adverbs*

Complete the following advert by translating the adverbs.

Keine schlaflosen Nächte mehr mit SOMNIUM!
Schlafen Sie [always] [well] oder liegen Sie [for hours] wach? Zählen Sie [at night] Schafe, statt [sweetly] zu träumen?

Mit SOMNIUM können Sie [immediately] einschlafen . . . das heißt, [in the morning] arbeiten Sie [very effectively] und [quickly], können [clearly] denken . . . und überhaupt [more carefree] leben!

▼ Order of adverbs

The order in which adverbs appear in an English sentence can vary:

I go to work by bus every morning.
Every morning I go to work by bus.
Every morning I go by bus to work.

In German, on the other hand, the adverbs normally come in a certain order:

1. Time (every morning) **2.** Manner (by bus) **3.** Place (to work). Remember **TMP**. The German must therefore be:

Ich fahre jeden Tag mit dem Bus zur Arbeit.

If you have two adverbs of the same type in a sentence, the more **general** one (the one that covers more time or space) comes first:

Sie trinkt Kaffee täglich um vier Uhr mit der Nachbarin.
Deine Brille liegt im Wohnzimmer auf dem Tisch.

▼ Activity 2   *Order of adverbs*

Translate the following sentences into German, making sure you put the adverbs in the right order.

1. I often walk [= go on foot] to the sports centre.
2. In summer the cat lies in the garden for hours.
3. We sometimes eat breakfast on the balcony.
4. Did you go to Austria by train last year?
5. We're going to meet in the café today at 4 o'clock.

▼ Comparisons with adverbs

Adverbs form their comparative and superlative forms in the same way as adjectives (see page 19):

Er ißt schnell.
Sein Bruder ißt schneller.
Der Hund ißt am schnellsten.

He eats quickly.
His brother eats more quickly.
The dog eats most quickly.

There are some irregular forms:

bald *(soon)*	früher	am frühesten
gern *(willingly)*	lieber *(rather)*	am liebsten
gut *(well)*	besser	am besten
oft *(often)*	öfter	am öftesten
viel *(a lot)*	mehr	am meisten

▼ Activity 3   *Comparisons with adverbs*

Complete the following conversation by translating the adverbs in brackets.

„Kannst du deine Musik nicht [more quietly] spielen? Es ist schon nach Mitternacht!"

„Das ist ein Scherz! In der Badewanne singst *du* doch [more loudly] als alle andere, besonders wenn *ich* [rather] schlafen würde."

„Morgen muß ich aber [earlier] aufstehen, verstehst du nicht?"

„Kannst du nicht [less aggressively] mit mir reden? Wenn du mich nur [more politely] fragen würdest . . ."

„Aber *du* bist der, der [most often] schreit, statt die Sache [more sensibly] zu diskutieren!"

„Ach, hör doch endlich auf. Wenn du [better] schlafen willst, nimm' doch eine Schlaftablette!"

PRONOUNS
replacing nouns

A pronoun is a word that is used instead of a noun. Pronouns can refer to people or things:

Meine Schwester wohnt in Hamburg. **Sie** studiert dort.
My sister lives in Hamburg. She is a student there.

Wer ist **der Mann** im Schwarz? Ich kenne **ihn** nicht.
Who is the man in black? I don't know him.

Gefällt dir **das Buch**? Ich habe **es** noch nicht gelesen.
Do you like the book? I haven't read it yet.

Since pronouns replace nouns, they change according to the part they play in the sentence:

Er trägt einen schwarzen Mantel. Ich kenne **ihn** nicht.
He's wearing a black coat. I don't know him.

The pronouns in the sentences above (he, she, him, it) are **personal** pronouns, replacing a person or thing. This is the type you will need most often. There are several other types: **reflexive** (myself, yourself), **indefinite** (one, something), **negative** (no-one, nothing), **possessive** (mine, yours), **interrogative** (who?, what?, which?), **relative** (who, which), and **demonstrative** (this one, that one).

▼ Activity 1   *Spot the pronoun*

Read the following passage carefully. It contains examples of different types of pronouns. Underline each one and say which type it is.

„Hallo Gabi! Hier ist die Karin. Ich gehe heute abend ins Kino. Kommst du mit? Oder hast du schon etwas vor?"

„Eigentlich nichts Besonderes. Was siehst du dir an? Wahrscheinlich etwas Verrücktes."

„Überhaupt nicht. Ich habe den Titel des Filmes vergessen, aber er geht um einen großen Liebhaber."

„Ah ja? Und wer spielt ihn?" ➤

„Niemand, den ich kenne."
„Also warum interessierst du dich dafür*?"
„Jemand hat mir davon* erzählt... Peter, der hat ihn gesehen."
„Okay. Soll ich dich abholen? Fahren wir mit meinem Auto?"
„Nein, nehmen wir lieber meines. Man weiß nie, ob man eine Fahrt mit dir überleben wird!"
„Das ist aber eine Frechheit!"

*dafür = 'in it'
*davon = 'about it'

▼ Personal pronouns

The conversation above included some examples of **direct object** pronouns in the accusative – 'Wer spielt **ihn**?' – and **indirect object** pronouns in the dative – 'Jemand hat **mir** davon erzählt'. The complete list is below.

	Person	Nom.	Acc.	Dat.
SINGULAR	1st (I)	ich	mich	mir
	2nd (you)	du	dich	dir
	3rd (he)	er	ihn	ihm
	(she)	sie	sie	ihr
	(it)	es	es	ihm
	(you-polite)	Sie	Sie	Ihnen
PLURAL	1st (we)	wir	uns	uns
	2nd (you)	ihr	euch	euch
	3rd (they)	sie	sie	ihnen
	(you-polite)	Sie	Sie	Ihnen

Remember to choose the correct pronoun for 'it': this depends on the gender of the thing being referred to:

Ich habe **den Tisch** nicht gekauft. **Er** war zu groß.
Ich habe **der Katze** etwas zu essen gegeben. **Sie** war hungrig.
Wieviel hat **das Auto** gekostet? **Es** sieht teuer aus.

■ **Du, ihr or Sie?**

You will have noticed the three forms for 'you'. 'Sie' is the polite form of address, used when talking to people over the age of 16 whom you don't know or haven't yet agreed to address as 'du' ('duzen'). 'Du' is used when speaking to children, God, animals, friends and family members, and among students. 'Ihr' is the plural form of 'du'. The general trend is for people of similar age to address each other as 'du', though it is wise to err on the side of politeness – if in doubt, use 'Sie'!

In letters, Du, Dich, etc. are written with capitals.

▼ *Word order*

In a sentence containing several nouns and pronouns as objects, they have to appear in a certain order:

• With two nouns, the **indirect** object comes first:

Ich lieh **meinem Bruder** das Auto.

• With one noun and one pronoun, the **pronoun** comes first:

Ich lieh **ihm** das Auto.
Ich lieh **es** meinem Bruder.

• With two pronouns, the **direct** object comes first:

Ich lieh **es** ihm.

▼ **Activity 2**   *Replace nouns with pronouns*

In the sentences below, change the nouns underlined into pronouns. Change the word order too where necessary.

1. Maria ist in die Stadt gefahren.
2. Sie schenkt ihrer Schwester ein Video.
3. Ich mag den Käse nicht.
4. Ich werde meinem Freund die ganze Geschichte erzählen.
5. Hast du den Kindern die Bücher gegeben?
6. Die Frau habe ich irgendwo gesehen.

■ **Damit or mit ihm?**

When a preposition is combined with a pronoun which is replacing a thing and not a person – 'on it' (the table), 'about it' (the film) – the two words are put together:

Das Buch liegt auf dem Tisch. Es liegt **darauf.**
Er erzählt mir von dem Film. Er erzählt mir **davon.**

Contrast 'Ich bin **mit ihm** gefahren' ('I went with him') and 'Ich bin **damit** gefahren ('I went with it', e.g. that train).

▼ Reflexive pronouns

Reflexive pronouns 'reflect back' to the subject. They are used mainly with reflexive verbs (see page 72) such as 'er hat **sich** wehgetan', 'he hurt himself'. However, they are also used when the person on the receiving end of an action is also the doer. In the sentence 'He shut the door behind him', you need to know whether the 'he' and the 'him' are the same person. If they are, you have to use a reflexive pronoun; if not, a personal pronoun.

- *The same person:* Er machte die Tür hinter **sich** zu.
- *A different person:* Er machte die Tür hinter **ihm** zu.

'He broke his leg' is expressed like this in German:

Er hat **sich das Bein** gebrochen.

'I broke my leg' is:

Ich habe **mir das Bein** gebrochen.

If you say 'Er hat **sein** Bein gebrochen', it means that he broke another person's leg!

Here is the complete list of reflexive pronouns:

	Person	Acc.	Dat.
SINGULAR	1st (ich)	mich	mir
	2nd (du)	dich	dir
	3rd (er/sie/es)	sich	sich
PLURAL	1st (wir)	uns	uns
	2nd (ihr)	euch	euch
	3rd (sie)	sich	sich
	(Sie)	sich	sich

▼ Indefinite pronouns

Words like 'one', 'no-one', 'someone' and 'something' are indefinite pronouns. They too **decline** according to their role in the sentence.

▼ *Man*

'Man' corresponds to the English 'one', meaning you, someone, or people in general.

In diesem Restaurant kann **man** sehr gut essen.
This restaurant is a good place to eat.

In Frankreich trinkt **man** viel Wein.
In France people drink a lot of wine.

Wie sagt **man** das auf deutsch?
How do you say that in German?

▼ *Einer, eine, eines* (one of)

This corresponds to the English 'one (of)'. Here are the forms:

	Masc.	Fem.	Neut.
Nom.	einer	eine	eines
Acc.	einen	eine	eines
Dat.	einem	einer	einem

Einer meiner Freunde kann japanisch.
One of my friends speaks Japanese.

Ich habe zwei Kopien davon – soll ich dir **eine** geben?
I've got two copies of it – shall I give you one?

In the plural you have to use 'welche':

Suchst du Tassen? Hier gibt's **welche**.
Are you looking for cups? There are some here.

▼ *Jemand (someone)*

Nom.	jemand
Acc.	jemand(en)
Dat.	jemand(em)

Ich sehe **jemand(en)** im Garten.
I can see someone in the garden.

▼ *Etwas (something)*
'Etwas' never changes:

Nom. Ist **etwas** passiert?   *Has something happened?*
Acc. Möchtest du **etwas** essen?   *Would you like something to eat?*

It can also be used with an adjective (see page 17).

▼ Negative pronouns

▼ *Keiner, keine, keines (none, not one, not any)*

	Masc.	Fem.	Neut.	Plural
Nom.	keiner	keine	keines	keine
Acc.	keinen	keine	keines	keine
Dat.	keinem	keiner	keinem	keinen

Darf ich deinen Regenschirm ausleihen? Ich habe **keinen**.
Can I borrow your umbrella? I haven't got one.

Ich habe mit **keinem** der Deutschen gesprochen.
I haven't spoken to any of the Germans.

▼ *Niemand (nobody)*
Nom. niemand
Acc. niemand(en)
Dat. niemand(em)

Ich habe einen Kuchen gebacken, aber **niemand** hat ihn gegessen.
I baked a cake, but no-one ate it.

Du darfst es **niemand(em)** sagen.
You mustn't tell anyone.

▼ *Nichts (nothing)*
Like 'etwas', this never changes:

Nom. **Nichts** ist passiert. Nothing has happened.
Acc. Ich habe **nichts** gehört. I haven't heard anything.
Dat. Sie haben mit **nichts** angefangen. They started with nothing.

'Nichts' can also be used with an adjective (see page 17).

▼ **Activity 3** *Indefinite and negative pronouns*

Choose one of these pronouns to fill in each gap: man, einer/eine/eines, jemand, etwas, keiner/keine/keines, niemand, nichts. Make sure each one is in the correct form.

6. Oktober

Ich bin in die Stadt gefahren, um ____ zu kaufen. Leider habe ich vergessen, was es war! Dann wollte ich ein Kochbuch kaufen, habe aber ____ gefunden. In der Buchhandlung hat mir ____ auf die Schulter geklopft – es war ____ meiner ehemaligen Schulkollegen! ____ hat mir gesagt, er sei im Ausland, aber ____ hat ____ von ihm gehört. Wir sind in ein Restaurant gegangen, wo ____ immer ____ Gutes zu essen bekommt. Ich war froh, ihn zu sehen. Er hat mir von ____ seiner vielen Abenteuer erzählt. Dann bin ich nach Hause gefahren – ohne ____ gekauft zu haben!

▼ Possessive pronouns

A possessive pronoun replaces the noun in phrases such as 'my book', 'your bag', 'our parents', 'her mistake':

Hast du **mein Buch** gesehen? Nein, hast du **meines** gesehen?
*Have you seen **my book**? No, have you seen **mine**?*

Ist das **meine Tasche**?
Ja, es ist **deine**.
*Is that **my bag**?*
*Yes, it's **yours**.*

Ich mag **deine Eltern** – **unsere** sind viel strenger!
*I like **your parents** – **ours** are much stricter!*

War es **sein Fehler** oder **ihrer**?
*Was it **his mistake** or **hers**?*

meiner, meine, mein(e)s	*mine*	unserer, unsere, unser(e)s	*ours*
deiner, deine, dein(e)s	*yours*	eurer, eu(e)re, euer(e)s	*yours*
seiner, seine, sein(e)s	*his*	Ihrer, Ihre, Ihr(e)s	*yours*
ihrer, ihre, ihr(e)s	*hers*	ihrer, ihre, ihr(e)s	*theirs*

You will come across meins, deins, etc. (without the 'e') in speech. These pronouns are declined like 'kein' (see page 33).

▼ Interrogative pronouns

Interrogative pronouns are those which ask a question – 'Wer?' ('Who?'), 'Was?' ('What?'), 'Welcher?' ('Which?'), 'Was für?' ('What sort of?').

▼ *Wer*

Nom.	wer	*who*
Acc.	wen	*whom*
Gen.	wessen	*whose*
Dat.	wem	*whom*

Wer ist noch gekommen?	*Who else came?*
Gegen **wen** spielt ihr?	*Who are you playing? (Against whom . . .)*
Wessen Mantel ist das?	*Whose coat is that?*
Wem schenkst du das?	*Who are you giving that to?*

▼ *Was/was für*

'Was' ('what') and 'was für' ('what sort of') are the same in the nominative and accusative:

Nom.	**Was** ist das?	*What's that?*
Acc.	**Was** hast du gegessen?	*What did you eat?*
Nom.	**Was für** ein Hund ist das?	*What sort of dog is that?*
Acc.	**Was für** ein Auto kaufst du?	*What sort of car are you buying?*

Remember that 'was für' is always followed by an indefinite article.

▼ *Welcher/welche/welches*

This asks the question 'which (one)?'. It declines as follows:

	Masc.	**Fem.**	**Neut.**	**Plural**
Nom.	welcher	welche	welches	welche
Acc.	welchen	welche	welches	welche
Dat.	welchem	welcher	welchem	welchen

Welcher von ihnen hat es getan?
Which one of them did it?

Ich habe zwei Bücher. **Welches** willst du lesen?
I've got two books. Which one do you want to read?

▼ **Activity 4**   *Possessive and interrogative pronouns*

Fill each gap with a suitable pronoun.

1. ____ rufst du an?
2. Sein Auto ist vielleicht größer, aber ____ ist bequemer.
3. Dieser Mantel gehört nicht mir. Ist er ____?
4. ____ Stimme ist das?
5. ____ Eis möchtest du?
6. ____ Film habt ihr gesehen?
7. Ist das mein Glas oder ____?
8. ____ willst du das Bild schenken? Meiner Mutter oder ____?

▼ **Activity 5**   *Asking questions*

Can you ask at least three questions, using the interrogative pronouns on page 35, to get more information about the following statements?
Example: Ich war in der Stadt.
In **welcher** Stadt warst du? **Was** hast du gemacht? **Wen** hast du getroffen?

1. Er fährt morgen nach Deutschland.
2. Wir waren gestern auf einer Party.
3. Sie hat ein Buch gekauft.
4. Ich möchte ins Kino gehen.

▼ Relative pronouns

Words like 'who', 'which', 'that' and 'whose' are relative pronouns. They 'relate' to a noun or idea earlier in the sentence:

Die Frau, **die** ich sah, hatte kurze, schwarze Haare.
The woman who I saw had short, black hair.

Das Haus, **von dem** du redest, ist schon verkauft worden.
The house which you're talking about has already been sold.

In English we could miss out the relative pronouns 'who' and 'which' in these examples, but in German you must **always** include them.

▼ *Der, die, das*

These are used for 'who(m)', 'that' or 'which'. They are declined as follows:

	Masc.	Fem.	Neut.	Plural
Nom.	der	die	das	die
Acc.	den	die	das	die
Gen.	dessen	deren	dessen	deren
Dat.	dem	der	dem	denen

As you can see, only the genitive forms and the dative plural are different from the normal forms of the definite article.

The relative pronoun agrees with the noun that goes before it in terms of **gender**. However, its **case** may be different. You can work this out from the part it plays in the **relative clause**, or part of the sentence in which it is contained.

Hast du **den Mann** gesehen, **der** nebenan wohnt?
Have you seen the man who lives next door?
(Den Mann = masculine accusative; der = masculine **but** nominative because the man is the subject in the relative clause.)

There are two other important points:

1. The verb is sent to the end in a relative clause (. . . der nebenan **wohnt**).
2. You must include a comma before the relative clause, or commas around the clause if it is in the middle of a sentence.

Here are some other examples:

Das Mädchen, **dessen** Fahrrad ich ausgeliehen habe, heißt Susanne.
The girl whose bicycle I borrowed is called Susanne.
(Das Mädchen = neuter nominative; dessen = neuter **but** genitive – **whose** bicycle.)

Deine Spende hilft **den Kindern, die** in der dritten Welt hungern.
Your donation helps the children who are starving in the Third World.
(den Kindern = dative plural; die = plural **but** nominative – they are starving.)

Die Firma, **bei der** ich jetzt arbeite, verkauft Computer.
The firm I'm now working for sells computers.
(die Firma = feminine nominative; der = feminine **but** dative after 'bei' – 'for which'.)

▼ *Was*

This can be used as a relative pronoun in the following ways:

Er sagte mir alles, **was** er wußte.
He told me everything (that) he knew.

Das ist das Größte, **was** ich habe.
That's the biggest (that) I have.

Sie gibt mir immer Obst aus dem Garten, **was** sehr nett von ihr ist.
She's always giving me fruit from the garden, (an action) which is very kind of her.

Das, **was** sie sagt, stimmt wirklich.
What she says is really true.

▼ Activity 6   *Relative pronouns*

Join the following pairs of sentences by using a relative pronoun. For example:
Sie hat einen neuen Freund. Er ist auch Student.
Sie hat einen neuen Freund, <u>der</u> auch Student ist.
Remember to think about a) gender, b) case, c) word order, and d) punctuation (commas).

1. Ich kenne eine interessante Frau. Sie ist Wissenschaftlerin.
2. Hast du mit dem Mann gesprochen? Sein Sohn arbeitet in Deutschland.
3. Ich habe am Wochenende Tennis gespielt. Es macht mir immer Spaß.
4. Wir haben in Hotels übernachtet. Sie waren ganz billig.
5. Er hat viel gesagt. Alles war interessant.
6. Sie spielen ein Lied. Das Lied gefällt mir sehr gut.
7. Ich fahre mit dem Zug. Er hat immer Verspätung.
8. Willst du das Buch lesen? Ich habe dir davon erzählt.

▼ Demonstrative pronouns

You need a demonstrative pronoun to say 'this one' and 'that one'. All the demonstrative adjectives (see page 18) can be used as pronouns, as can der/die/das in conversational German or to give special emphasis:

Die ist eine mutige Frau!
She's a brave woman!

Den kenne ich nicht.
I don't know him.

Dieses ist zwar billiger, aber **jenes** gefällt mir besser.
This one's cheaper, but I prefer that one.

Jeder mag ihn.
Everyone likes him.

PREPOSITIONS
position and relation of things

Prepositions go before a noun or pronoun and indicate the relationship between it and the rest of the sentence. Many prepositions describe the position of something or someone in space (on, in, at) or time (before, during, after).

Der Schlüssel liegt **auf** dem Tisch.
The key is on the table.

Ich werde sie **nach** dem Mittagessen anrufen.
I'll phone her after lunch.

As in English, many prepositions are used after verbs: to think **about** (denken **an**), to rely **on** (sich verlassen **auf**). As well as learning which preposition to use – it's not always the same one as in English – you need to know which **case** it takes.

Ich dachte **an meinen Urlaub.** *(an + accusative)*
I thought about my holiday.

Some prepositions always take the same case, but others can take two (see page 42).

▼ Activity 1   *Spot the preposition*

Read the following passage and underline each preposition. Identify which case it takes if you can.

„Meine Damen und Herren, in wenigen Minuten werden wir in Heathrow landen. Wegen der starken Winde während des Flugs haben wir leider eine kleine Verspätung. Bitte kehren Sie zu Ihrem Platz zurück und schnallen Sie sich an. Stellen Sie Ihr Handgepäck unter den Sitz vor Ihnen. Achten Sie bitte darauf, daß Ihr Sitz aufrecht ist, und daß der Tisch vor Ihnen hochgeklappt ist.
Von der linken Seite des Flugzeugs können Sie Big Ben und die Houses of Parliament sehen. Das Wetter in London ist sonnig. Es hat über zwanzig Grad. Die Ortszeit ist fünf Minuten nach vier.
Im Namen von Flugkapitän Smith und seiner Besatzung möchte ich Ihnen einen angenehmen Aufenthalt in England wünschen und mich bei Ihnen bedanken, daß Sie unsere Fluglinie gewählt haben."

- These prepositions always take the **accusative**:

durch	*through*
ohne	*without*
gegen	*against, towards*
wider	*against* (only used in certain phrases, see page 48)
um	*round*
für	*for*

It may help if you remember DOGWUF!
Entlang (along) also takes the accusative, but it usually goes after its noun:

Er ging den Fluß entlang.
He walked along the river.

Bis (by, until) takes the accusative:

Kannst du es bis nächsten Montag fertig haben?
Can you have it done by next Monday?

However, it is more often used together with another preposition: bis auf (+ accusative), except for; bis zu (+ dative), up to.

- These prepositions always take the **genitive**:

außerhalb	*outside*
diesseits	*on this side of*
innerhalb	*inside*
jenseits	*on the other side of*
nördlich	*north of*
statt	*instead of*
südlich	*south of*
trotz	*in spite of*
während	*during*
wegen	*because of*

- These prepositions always take the **dative**:

aus	*out of, from*
außer	*except*
bei	*at*
mit	*with*
nach	*to, after*
seit	*since*
von	*from, of*
zu	*to*

'Gegenüber' ('opposite') and 'entgegen' ('towards') also take
the dative, but normally go after their noun:

Wir wohnen der Schule **gegenüber**.
We live opposite the school.

Er kam mir **entgegen**.
He came towards me.

- These prepositions can take the **accusative OR dative**:

an	*on (the side of)*
auf	*on (the top of)*
hinter	*behind*
in	*in*
neben	*near, next to*
über	*over, across*
unter	*under, among*
vor	*in front of, before*
zwischen	*between*

They take the **accusative** if they show **motion** to a place:

Sie gehen **in den** Garten.   *They're going into the garden.*
Das Auto fuhr **hinter das** Haus.   *The car drove behind the house.*

They take the **dative** if there is **no motion** involved:

Sie sitzen **im** Garten.   *They're sitting in the garden.*
Das Auto steht **hinter dem** Haus.   *The car's behind the house.*

and also if the motion takes place on the spot!

Sie spielten Tennis **im** Park.
They were playing tennis in the park.

As was mentioned on page 2, some prepositions are often
combined with the definite article so that 'in dem' becomes
'im', for example. Unless you want to stress the article, as in
the second example below, you should use the contracted form,
zum – it sounds more natural.

Ich gehe **zum** Supermarkt.
I'm going to the supermarket.

Warum gehst du **zu dem** Supermarkt? Der andere ist doch billiger.
*Why do you go to **that** supermarket? The other one is cheaper.*

▼ Activity 2   *Accusative or dative?*

Should the prepositions in the following passage take the accusative or the dative? In each case, choose the correct version.

Lieber Andreas!
Das ganze Essen habe ich in den/im Kühlschrank gestellt. Den Salat kannst du einfach in eine andere/einer anderen Schüssel tun; Teller fürs Brot findest du in den/dem Regal. Stell' bitte ein paar Flaschen Wein auf den/dem Tisch neben die Gläser/den Gläsern.

Hinter den/dem CD-Spieler gibt's eine Schachtel mit CDs – such' dir etwas aus. Ich habe schon alles aufgeräumt – das heißt, ich habe meine ganzen Sachen unter das/dem Sofa gestopft!

Ich komme um sieben – hoffentlich vor die Gäste/den Gästen . . .
Bis später,
Martina

▼ Other uses of prepositions

As well as describing position in space or time, many prepositions are used in phrases with nouns, verbs and adjectives to express less 'concrete' relationships. As you'll see, in many cases the German phrase uses a different preposition from the English or includes a preposition when the English doesn't. The list below combines these uses of prepositions with other set phrases of place and time where the preposition differs from English usage.

▼ *An + accusative*

gewohnt an	*accustomed to*
denken an	*to think of*
sich erinnern an	*to remember*
sich gewöhnen an	*to get used to*
Er kommt an die Reihe.	*It's his turn.*

▼ *An + dative*

am Morgen, Nachmittag, usw.	*in the morning, afternoon, etc.*
Schuld an	*guilty of*
arbeiten an	*to work on*
leiden an	*to suffer from*
teilnehmen an	*to take part in*

▼ *Auf + accusative*

aufs Land gehen	to go into the country
auf diese Weise	in this way
auf jeden Fall	in any case
auf deutsch	in German
die Antwort auf	the answer to
stolz auf	proud of
böse auf	angry with
achten/aufpassen auf	to pay attention to
antworten auf	to answer (a question)
sich freuen auf	to look forward to
hoffen auf	to hope for
warten auf	to wait for
sich verlassen auf	to rely on
weisen/zeigen auf	to point to

▼ *Auf + dative*

auf dem Bahnhof	at the station
auf dem Land	in the country
auf der Straße	in the street
auf dem Weg	on the way

▼ *Aus + dative*

Er kommt/stammt aus Berlin.	He comes from Berlin.
aus Holz, usw	made of wood, etc
bestehen aus	to consist of

▼ *Außer + dative*

Außer dir sehe ich niemand.	I see nobody except you.
Sie ist außer Atem.	She is out of breath.

▼ *Bei + dative*

Er wohnt bei seinen Eltern.	He lives with his parents.
bei schlechtem Wetter	in bad weather
bei seiner Ankunft/Rückkehr	on his arrival/return
Er hat kein Geld bei sich.	He has no money on him.
bei Tagesanbruch	at daybreak
bei Sonnenuntergang	at sunset
sich beklagen bei	to complain to
sich entschuldigen bei	to apologise to
helfen bei	to help with

▼ *Bis + accusative*

Sie bleiben bis Ostern.	*They're staying till Easter.*
Bis nächsten Sonntag ist er zurück.	*He'll be back by next Sunday.*
neun bis zehn Jahre	*nine to ten years*

▼ *Durch + accusative*

Ich wurde durch den Lärm geweckt.	*I was awoken by the noise.*

▼ *Für + accusative*

Er tat es für mich.	*He did it for me.*
danken für	*to thank for*
sich interessieren für	*to be interested in*
schwärmen für	*to be very keen on*
sorgen für	*to look after*
halten für	*to consider*
Ich halte ihn für einen Narren.	*I think he's a fool.*

▼ *Gegen + accusative*

Er schwimmt gegen den Strom.	*He's swimming against the current.*
gegen 4 Uhr	*about 4 o'clock*
Ich habe nichts dagegen.	*I've nothing against that.*

▼ *In + accusative*

ins Ausland reisen	*to go abroad*
ins Freie gehen	*to go outside*
ins Theater/Kino usw gehen	*to go to the theatre/cinema etc*
in Ordnung bringen	*to tidy, repair, sort out*
sich verlieben in	*to fall in love with*

▼ *In + dative*

in der Nähe von	*near*
im Freien sein	*to be in the open air*
in der Nacht	*at night*
in dem Augenblick	*at that moment*
einmal im Jahr	*once a year*
im Gegenteil	*on the contrary*
im allgemeinen	*in general*
im Radio/Fernsehen	*on the radio/television*
ankommen in	*to arrive at*

▼ *Mit + dative*

mit dem Auto usw	*by car etc*
Ich habe es mit der Post geschickt.	*I sent it by post.*
mit leiser Stimme	*in a quiet voice*
sich beschäftigen mit	*to be busy with*
sprechen mit	
sich unterhalten mit	*to talk to*

▼ *Nach + dative*

Er kam nach Hause.	*He arrived home.*
meiner Meinung nach	*in my opinion*
in der Richtung nach	*in the direction of*
sich erkundigen nach	*to enquire about*
fragen nach	*to ask about*
schmecken nach	*to taste of*
riechen nach	*to smell of*

▼ *Seit + dative*

seit dem Krieg	*since the war*
Ich lerne Deutsch seit zwei Jahren.*	*I have been learning German for two years.*
Ich wartete seit langem.*	*I had been waiting for a long time.*

* Notice the use of the present and imperfect tenses in these two examples (see page 80).

▼ *Über + accusative*

Sie fuhr über Berlin.	*She went via Berlin.*
ein Bericht über	*a report on*
traurig über	*sad about*
enttäuscht über	*disappointed in*
zornig über	*angry at*
sich beklagen über	*to complain about*
sich freuen über	*to be glad about*
nachdenken über	*to reflect, think over*
klagen über	*to complain of*
lachen über	*to laugh at*
sich wundern über	*to be surprised at, puzzled about*
schreiben über	*to write about*

▼ *Um + accusative*

um 4 Uhr	*at 4 o'clock*
um so besser	*all the better*
um so mehr	*all the more*
bitten um	*to ask for*
sich kümmern um	*to worry about*
sich bewerben um	*to apply for*

▼ *Unter + dative*

unter den Kindern	*among the children*
unter anderem	*among other things*
unter diesen Umständen	*in these circumstances*
unter uns	*amongst ourselves, between you and me*

▼ *Von + dative*

von Zeit zu Zeit	*from time to time*
von nun an	*from now on*
handeln von	*to be about*
nördlich (usw) von	*to the north (etc) of*
erzählen von	*to tell of/about*
abhängen von	*to depend on*
sprechen von	*to talk of*
Ich lese einen Roman von Thomas Mann.	*I'm reading a novel by Thomas Mann.*

▼ *Vor + dative*

vor einem Jahr	*a year ago*
vor langer Zeit	*a long time ago*
vor allem	*above all*
sicher vor	*safe from*
Angst haben vor } sich fürchten vor	*to be afraid of*
vor Freude lachen	*to laugh with joy*
schützen vor	*to protect from*
warnen vor	*to warn against*

▼ *Wegen + genitive*

berühmt wegen	*famous for*
sich schämen wegen	*to be ashamed of*

▼ *Wider + accusative*

'Gegen' is used to mean opposition to something physical.
'Wider' shows opposition to something mental or moral.

Er tat es wider meinen Willen.	*He did it against my wishes.*
wider Willen	*reluctantly*

▼ *Zu + dative*

zur Schule	*to school*
Er ging zu Bett.	*He went to bed.*
zu Hause	*at home*
zu Fuß	*on foot*
zu Ostern, Weihnachten	*at Easter, Christmas*
zu der Zeit	*at that time*
zu beiden Seiten	*on both sides*
Die Schuhe passen nicht zum Kleid.	*The shoes don't match/go with the dress.*
zum Glück	*luckily*
zum Beispiel	*for example*
das Gasthaus zum Löwen	*the 'Lion' inn*
gehören zu	*to belong to (i.e. be part of)*
eine Briefmarke zu 2 DM	*a two-mark stamp*

▼ Activity 3   *Which preposition?*

Translate the following sentences into German, a) choosing the correct preposition and b) deciding which case should be used after it.

1. Would you like to take part in a play?
2. They helped me with the washing up.
3. We bought a new car a few days ago.
4. Many passengers complained about the delay.
5. Are you interested in football?
6. When it was his turn, he bought a ticket to Berlin.
7. I bought two CDs for £10.99 each.
8. He parked his car near the station.
9. In my opinion the minister should resign [zurücktreten].
10. She's so proud of herself!

VERBS
saying what is happening

Verbs are the key words in any language. They are 'where the action is': they enable you to say what is being done and by whom.

Verbs change according to:

• who the subject is:

Sie fragt	*She asks*
Wir fragen	*We ask*

In other words they have to **agree** with the subject.

• when the action takes place – in the past, present, or future – in other words, which **tense** you are using.

Sie fragt	*She asks (present)*
Sie fragte	*She asked (past – imperfect tense)*
Sie wird fragen	*She will ask (future)*

▼ 'Strong' and 'weak' verbs

German verbs are divided into two groups – strong and weak. The **weak** verbs are also known as 'regular' verbs because they follow a regular pattern. **Strong** verbs are 'irregular' – they do their own thing, having their own pattern which doesn't follow the regular rules. We have these differences in English too but we don't need to think about them. For example, 'swim' and 'sing' don't follow the usual rule of adding 'ed' in the past tense, but change to 'swam' and 'sang'. Similar changes take place in German and need to be learned. Some common verbs are irregular in both languages – swim (schwimmen), bring (bringen) and find (finden) are just three examples.

So, to know the right forms of a German verb, we need to know if it is weak or strong. There is a list of the most common strong verbs on pages 99–102 to help you. If the verb you are looking for is not in the list, treat it as a weak (regular) verb. There are also some 'mixed' verbs (see page 54).

▼ *The infinitive*

Before we look at each of the tenses, we need to be able to recognise the most basic form of the verb, and the form which is given in the dictionary – the **infinitive**.

If you look up 'catch' and 'find' in an English/German dictionary, you'll find 'fangen' and 'finden'. These are the 'infinitives', 'to catch' and 'to find'.

In German each infinitive consists of two parts – the 'stem' and the 'ending'. The 'ending' is usually -en:

Stem **Ending**
↓   ↓
fang**en**
find**en**

Sometimes the ending is only -n:

Stem **Ending**
↓   ↓
wander**n**
sammel**n**

Knowing about the 'stem' and the 'ending' enables you to form the different parts of the verb.

▼ The present tense

The present tense in German is used for:

- describing a state in the present: I live in London.
- describing an action going on now: He's painting the ceiling.
- describing something done regularly: We play football on Sundays.
- talking about future events: The plane leaves at 2.
- describing an action which started in the past and is still going on now: I've been learning German for two years.

To form the present tense, you take the stem of the verb and add the following endings:

ich	E	wir	EN
du	ST	ihr	T
er		sie	EN
sie	T	Sie	EN
es			
Sie	EN		

So 'kaufen' is:

ich kauf**e**	wir kauf**en**
du kauf**st**	ihr kauf**t**
er	sie kauf**en**
sie } kauf**t**	Sie kauf**en**
es	
Sie kauf**en**	

If the stem of the verb ends in 'd', 'n' or 't', you add an 'e' so that the word is easier to pronounce: reden (du redest), öffnen (du öffnest), arbeiten (du arbeitest). If the stem ends in 's', you simply add 't' to the 'du' form: reisen (du reist), heißen (du heißt).

▼ Activity 1   *Subject–verb agreement*

Complete the crossword below by translating the verbs into German.

Waagerecht
  1. [They] mix
  3. [He] is looking for
  4. [I] sew
  5. [We] do
  7. [I] am drinking
  9. [She] fills
 10. [You – polite] stand

Senkrecht
  1. [You] are doing
  2. [I] harm
  3. [They] send
  4. [He] names
  6. [It] goes
  8. [You] call

We've already talked about 'weak' (regular) and 'strong' (irregular) verbs. Some strong verbs change their stem vowel in the du and er/sie/es forms. 'I catch' is 'ich fange' – the stem plus the ending. 'You catch', however, is 'du fängst' and 'he catches' is 'er fängt' – the 'a' changes to 'ä'. The endings are the same. Other examples are:

sehen: ich sehe, du **siehst**
sprechen: ich spreche, du **sprichst**

There is a list of strong verbs on pages 99–102 which shows these changes. The verbs sein (to be), haben (to have) and werden (to become) are also irregular. Since they are needed so often, they are written out in full on pages 59–60.

▼ Activity 2   *Present tense*

Complete the following passage, adding the correct forms of the verbs in brackets. Look at the list on pages 99-102 if necessary to find out if the verb you need is weak or strong.

„Du [sein] so faul! Du [denken] nie an andere Leute. Du [kommen] nach Hause, [lesen] die Zeitung, [helfen] mir nicht bei dem Abendessen und [waschen] nie ab. Du [machen] überhaupt keine Hausarbeit. Dann [sehen] du den ganzen Abend fern oder du [fahren] in die Stadt und [trinken] zu viel Bier!"

▼ The imperfect tense

The imperfect tense is used to **write** about past events, or when speaking in a more formal or distanced way about the past, such as in a news report or an account of childhood. It is used for both completed and continuing actions in the past: 'er suchte es' can mean both 'he looked for it' and 'he was looking for it'. Weak and strong verbs form this tense in different ways.

▼ *(a) Weak verbs*

The stems of these take the following endings:

ich	TE	wir	TEN
du	TEST	ihr	TET
er		sie	TEN
sie }	TE	Sie	TEN
es			
Sie	TEN		

So the imperfect forms of 'kaufen' are:

ich kaufte	wir kauften
du kauftest	ihr kauftet
er	sie kauften
sie } kaufte	Sie kauften
es	
Sie kauften	

If the stem already ends in 't' (e.g. warten) you need to add an 'e': ich wartete.

▼ *(b) Strong verbs*

In this case the **stem vowel** changes, not just the ending; just as English 'catch' changes to 'caught' and 'buy' to 'bought'. German examples are 'gehen', which changes to 'ging' and 'ziehen' which changes to 'zog'. This is the 'new stem' for the imperfect. To this new stem you add these endings:

ich	–	wir	EN
du	ST	ihr	T
er		sie	EN
sie }	–	Sie	EN
es			
Sie	EN		

So the imperfect forms of 'gehen' are:

ich ging	wir gingen
du gingst	ihr gingt
er	sie gingen
sie } ging	Sie gingen
es	
Sie gingen	

▼ *(c) Mixed verbs*

These take weak endings (see 'kaufen' above) but change the stem vowel as strong verbs do. Here is an example – 'rennen':

ich rannte	wir rannten
du ranntest	ihr ranntet
er ⎫	sie rannten
sie ⎬ rannte	Sie rannten
es ⎭	
Sie rannten	

Others are bringen, denken, brennen, kennen and senden.

▼ Activity 3   *Imperfect tense*

Turn the monologue in Activity 2 into a report in the imperfect tense, beginning with 'Er war so faul! . . .'

▼ The perfect tense

The perfect tense is used in conversation, when writing informally – such as in a letter to a friend – or describing the very recent past:

Hast du schon **gefrühstückt?**
Have you had breakfast yet?

Ich **bin** nach Deutschland **gefahren.**
I've been to Germany.

As in English, the perfect is made up of two parts:

1. the present tense of haben or sein (ich habe or ich bin)
2. the past participle (gefrühstückt/gefahren)

As these example sentences show, the past participle goes to the end of the sentence. To form the past participle, you need to know if the verb is weak or strong.

▼ *(a) Weak verbs*

Add ge- to the front of the stem and -t to the end. Kaufen (stem 'kauf') becomes gekauft and spielen (stem 'spiel') gespielt.

If the stem ends in 'd', 'n' or 't', you have to add an 'e': geredet, geöffnet, gearbeitet.

▼ (b) Strong verbs
Just as with the imperfect, you'll have to look on pages 99–102 to find these past participles – until you've learnt them all! For example, 'sein' becomes 'gewesen' and 'gehen' becomes 'gegangen'.

▼ (c) Mixed verbs
Mixed verbs are subject to the same stem vowel changes as strong verbs, but their past participles are regular and end in 't', like those of weak verbs:

brennen – gebrannt   bringen – gebracht   denken – gedacht

■ Other past participles
If the verb begins with be-, ent-, emp-, er-, ver- or zer-, or is a foreign loan word such as stud**ieren**, interess**ieren** or pass**ieren**, there is no ge- in the past participle, e.g. verkaufen becomes verkauft and studieren becomes studiert. If the verb has a separable prefix, e.g. wehtun (see page 69 for separable verbs), the ge- goes between the prefix and the main part of the verb: ich habe mich weh**ge**tan.

▼ Activity 4   *Perfect tense*

Complete the following conversation by putting the verbs in brackets into the perfect tense. Make sure the word order is correct.

„Was [machen] du am Wochenende?"
„Leider nichts Interessantes. Ich [putzen]."
„Ach, nein. Warum denn?"
„Meine Mutter [besuchen] mich. Sie [mitbringen] einen guten Kuchen, aber sonst war es schrecklich. Sie [fragen] die ganze Zeit, 'Warum [stellen] du das dort? Warum [tapezieren] du noch nicht? Warum [kaufen] du dir solche komischen Möbel ...?'"
„Und was [sagen] du dazu?"
„'Ich [haben] sehr wenig Zeit. In den letzten Wochen [lernen] ich sehr viel und [interessieren] mich überhaupt nicht für Hausarbeit.' Dann [geben] sie mir ein Kochbuch."
„Und du [sich aufregen] bestimmt!"

▼ *Haben or sein?*

All the verbs in activity 4 used haben to form their perfect tense. How do you know whether to use haben or sein?

If the verb is **transitive**, you use haben. If it is **intransitive** and shows a change of place or state, use sein. This is explained below!

Transitive verbs have a direct object; the action of the verb is 'done to' something. In 'Ich lese ein Buch' and 'er spielt Tennis', the book and tennis are the objects. If in doubt, check in the dictionary: transitive verbs are often indicated by 'v. tr'. Transitive verbs take haben:

Ich habe ein Buch gelesen.
Er hat Tennis gespielt.

Compare these sentences:

• *They have gone to Italy.*

What 'gets gone'? Nothing. There is no direct object, so the verb is intransitive. There is also a change of place involved. The verb therefore takes sein:

Sie **sind** nach Italien gefahren.

• *The cat appeared the next day.*

What 'gets appeared'? Nothing. No direct object, so the verb is intransitive. The German would be:

Die Katze **ist** am nächsten Tag aufgetaucht.

If you can sensibly ask and answer the 'what' question, then it's a transitive verb. If you can't, it's intransitive. Intransitive verbs are often indicated by 'v. intr.' in the dictionary.

▼ Activity 5   *Transitive or intransitive?*

Are the verbs underlined in these sentences transitive or intransitive?

1. Der Junge <u>fällt</u> in den Fluß.
2. Sie <u>bauen</u> ihr eigenes Haus.
3. Viele Soldaten <u>sterben</u> im Krieg.
4. Er <u>kauft</u> eine Zeitung.
5. Sie <u>gibt</u> dem Kind einen Apfel.
6. Sie <u>zieht</u> aus der Wohnung aus.

You'll find that the category of verbs taking sein consists of verbs of **movement** (laufen, aufstehen), but also bleiben (to stay) and sein (to be) – which could be described as verbs of existence. It also includes verbs such as aufwachen (to wake up) and einschlafen (to fall asleep) which express a change of state.

You can use a flow chart to help you decide between haben and sein.

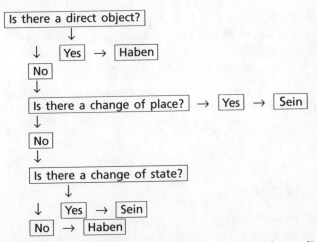

Some verbs can take either haben or sein depending on the meaning. 'Fahren' is an example:

Er ist nach Schottland gefahren.   *He's gone to Scotland (intransitive).*

Er hat das neue Auto gefahren.   *He drove the new car (transitive: das Auto is the object).*

▼ Activity 6 *Haben or sein?*

Complete the postcard below, putting the verbs in brackets into the perfect tense with haben or sein as appropriate.

Grüsse aus Griechenland!
Gestern [besuchen] wir diese Insel.
Wir [fahren] zwei Stunden mit dem
Boot, [steigen] dann auf einen Berg.
Wir [bewundern] die Aussicht und
[einschlafen]! Später [schwimmen]
wir im Meer und [sitzen] in der
Sonne. Die Zeit [vergehen] sehr
schnell... Leider [bekommen] ich
eine sehr rote Nase.
Alles Gute
Helmut und Klara

An die Familie Neumann
Virchowstr. 22
8901 Stadtbergen
Deutschland

▼ The pluperfect tense

The pluperfect describes an action in the past which was completed before another began. It is formed with the imperfect tense of haben or sein and the past participle. It is most often used together with a verb in the perfect or imperfect:

Ich **hatte** die Kekse schon **gegessen**, also habe ich den Kuchen probiert.
I had already eaten the biscuits, so I tried the cake.

Sie **war** schon **weggefahren**, als ich ankam.
She had already left when I arrived.

▼ The future tense

German has only one future form. It can express the English 'I will do something' as well as 'I'm going to do something'. It is made up of two parts:

1. the present tense of werden
2. the infinitive of the verb.

Just like the past participle, the infinitive goes to the end of the sentence.

The present tense of werden is:

ich	werde	wir	werden
du	wirst	ihr	werdet
er		sie	werden
sie ⎫	wird	Sie	werden
es ⎬			
Sie ⎭	werden		

A couple of examples:

Er **wird** dich morgen **anrufen**.   *He'll phone you tomorrow.*
Ich **werde** ein neues Auto **kaufen**.   *I'm going to buy a new car.*

▼ Activity 7   *Forming the future*

Put the following sentences into the future tense. Remember that the infinitive has to go to the end.

1. Sie kommt spät nach Hause.
2. Du bekommst einen Sonnenbrand!
3. Wir gehen ins Kino.
4. Ich koche Suppe.
5. Ihr macht zuviel Lärm.

As in English, the future is often also expressed by using the present tense:

Mein Zug **fährt** um sieben **ab**.   *My train leaves at seven.*
Ich **gehe** morgen ins Kino.   *I'm going to the cinema tomorrow.*

▼ Sein, haben and werden

You'll have noticed that several tenses are formed by using different tenses of sein (to be), haben (to have) and werden (to become). These are probably the most common verbs in German, so they are listed below for reference:

	Present	Imperfect	Perfect	Pluperfect
Sein				
ich	bin	war	bin gewesen	war gewesen
du	bist	warst	bist gewesen	warst gewesen
er, sie, es	ist	war	ist gewesen	war gewesen
Sie	sind	waren	sind gewesen	waren gewesen

	Present	Imperfect	Perfect	Pluperfect
wir	sind	waren	sind gewesen	waren gewesen
ihr	seid	wart	seid gewesen	wart gewesen
sie, Sie	sind	waren	sind gewesen	waren gewesen

Haben

	Present	Imperfect	Perfect	Pluperfect
ich	habe	hatte	habe gehabt	hatte gehabt
du	hast	hattest	hast gehabt	hattest gehabt
er, sie, es	hat	hatte	hat gehabt	hatte gehabt
Sie	haben	hatten	haben gehabt	hatten gehabt
wir	haben	hatten	haben gehabt	hatten gehabt
ihr	habt	hattet	habt gehabt	hattet gehabt
sie, Sie	haben	hatten	haben gehabt	hatten gehabt

Werden

	Present	Imperfect	Perfect	Pluperfect
ich	werde	wurde	bin geworden	war geworden
du	wirst	wurdest	bist geworden	warst geworden
er, sie, es	wird	wurde	ist geworden	war geworden
Sie	werden	wurden	sind geworden	waren geworden
wir	werden	wurden	sind geworden	waren geworden
ihr	werdet	wurdet	seid geworden	wart geworden
sie, Sie	werden	wurden	sind geworden	waren geworden

▼ The subjunctive

All the verbs we have met so far have been in the **indicative** mood: this means that they express **reality**. The **subjunctive**, on the other hand, is used to express **possibility**. It is not used much in English, except in certain phrases – 'If I were you . . .', 'God bless you'. In German it's used in conditional sentences (see below), in reported speech and in some phrases expressing wishes and uncertainty.

Can you see the difference in these two English sentences, even though the verbs ('lived' and 'could go swimming') are the same in both?

• When I lived at the seaside, I could go swimming every day. (You did live at the seaside – you were able to go swimming every day – fact – so indicative.)

• If I lived at the seaside, I could go swimming every day. (You don't live at the seaside – going swimming is only a possibility – so subjunctive.)

The last example is a conditional or 'wenn' sentence (see page 62).

▼ *The present subjunctive*

This is formed by putting endings onto stems. Weak and strong verbs have the same endings, which are:

ich	E	wir	EN
du	EST	ihr	ET
er		sie	EN
sie	E	Sie	EN
es			
Sie	EN		

So the present subjunctive of gehen is:

ich gehe	wir gehen
du gehest	ihr gehet
er	sie gehen
sie gehe	Sie gehen
es	
Sie gehen	

The er/sie/es form is the one you will encounter or need to use most often. It's helpful to remember that this is the same as the first person singular indicative.

▼ *The imperfect subjunctive*

Here you do have to know if a verb is weak or strong. The imperfect subjunctive of weak verbs is the same as the indicative. For strong verbs – which change in the imperfect – take the new imperfect stem and add an umlaut if the vowel is 'a', 'o' or 'u'. Thus the new stem for geben is gäb, and for sehen it's säh. The endings are the same as those for the present subjunctive. So geben (new stem gäb) is:

ich gäbe	wir gäben
du gäbest	ihr gäbet
er	sie gäben
sie gäbe	Sie gäben
es	
Sie gäben	

The subjunctive is used mainly in the present and imperfect. However, by using the present or imperfect subjunctive of haben, sein or werden and the past participle or infinitive, other tenses can be formed.

Since sein, haben and werden are so important, here are their subjunctive forms:

	Present	Imperfect	Perfect	Pluperfect
Sein				
ich	sei	wäre	sei gewesen	wäre gewesen
du	seiest	wärest	seiest gewesen	wärest gewesen
er, sie, es	sei	wäre	sei gewesen	wäre gewesen
Sie	seien	wären	seien gewesen	wären gewesen
wir	seien	wären	seien gewesen	wären gewesen
ihr	seiet	wäret	seiet gewesen	wäret gewesen
sie, Sie	seien	wären	seien gewesen	wären gewesen
Haben				
ich	habe	hätte	habe gehabt	hätte gehabt
du	habest	hättest	habest gehabt	hättest gehabt
er, sie, es	habe	hätte	habe gehabt	hätte gehabt
Sie	haben	hätten	haben gehabt	hätten gehabt
wir	haben	hätten	haben gehabt	hätten gehabt
ihr	habet	hättet	habet gehabt	hättet gehabt
sie, Sie	haben	hätten	haben gehabt	hätten gehabt
Werden				
ich	werde	würde	sei geworden	wäre geworden
du	werdest	würdest	seiest geworden	wärest geworden
er, sie, es	werde	würde	sei geworden	wäre geworden
Sie	werden	würden	seien geworden	wären geworden
wir	werden	würden	seien geworden	wären geworden
ihr	werdet	würdet	seiet geworden	wäret geworden
sie, Sie	werden	würden	seien geworden	wären geworden

▼ *Uses of the subjunctive*

■ 1 Conditional sentences

These are sometimes called 'wenn' sentences as they use the word 'wenn'. Some of these express possibilities, and they're the ones we use the subjunctive in. Look at the English meanings and you'll see which are facts (wenn = when/whenever) and which are possibilities (wenn = if/whether). They can be divided into four types.

(a) Wenn ich müde **bin, gehe** ich zu Bett.
 If (= when) I am tired I go to bed.
(b) Wenn ich müde **bin, werde** ich zu Bett **gehen**.
 If (= when) I am tired I'll go to bed.

(c) Wenn ich müde **wäre,**   (i) **würde** ich zu Bett **gehen.**

(ii) **ginge** ich zu Bett.

If I were tired I would go to bed.

(d) Wenn ich müde **gewesen wäre, wäre** ich zu Bett **gegangen.**

If I had been tired I would have gone to bed.

a and b are **facts,** so the verbs are indicative.

c and d are **possibilities** (c in the present, while d was a past possibility) so the verbs are subjunctive.

In c you can either use the conditional ('ich würde' – 'I would' plus infinitive) or the imperfect subjunctive. You must use the conditional if the imperfect subjunctive and indicative are the same, e.g. with weak verbs (see page 61).

Notice that the verb goes to the end after 'wenn'.

▼ Activity 8   *Conditional sentences*

Can you make up a, b, c and d sentences using the following statements? Then translate your sentences into English.

1. Ich bin durstig. Ich trinke eine Tasse Tee.
2. Sie hat Hunger. Sie ißt ein Käsebrot.
3. Wir langweilen uns. Wir sehen fern.
4. Es regnet. Die Kinder bleiben zu Hause.

■ 2 Indirect speech and question

Direct speech is what is actually said, whereas we use indirect speech to **report** what is said – which is why it is also known as reported speech.

• Direct speech: 'I'm going home,' he said.

Indirect speech: He said (that) he was going home.

• Direct question: 'When did you visit Germany?'

Indirect question: He asked me when I had visited Germany.

Did you notice what happened to the verbs when the English changed from 'direct' to 'indirect' speech? They moved back a tense. 'Am going' became 'was going' and 'visited' became 'had visited'. This isn't the case in German unless the indicative and subjunctive forms are the same:

Direct   • Er sagte: „Ich gehe nach Hause."

• Er fragte mich: „Wann haben Sie Deutschland besucht?"

Indirect   • Er sagte, er **gehe** nach Hause.

We can keep the verb in the present tense because 'geht' and 'gehe' are different.

• Er fragte mich, wann ich Deutschland besucht **hätte**.

We have to go back a tense so that the verb can clearly be seen to be a subjunctive. (The present subjunctive would be 'habe', the same as the present indicative.)

You can also include 'that' in an indirect statement ('He said **that** he was going home') and in this case the 'daß' sends the verb to the end:

Er sagte, **daß** er nach Hause gehe.

There are two important points to note about indirect questions: the verb goes to the end and the word for 'if' or 'whether' is 'ob':

Er fragte mich, **ob** ich Deutschland besucht hätte.

▼ **Activity 9** *Indirect speech and questions*

Turn the following conversation into indirect speech and questions. Remember to use an appropriate introductory verb (Er/sie sagte/fragte) and to pay attention to the word order.

„Die Theaterkarten waren zu teuer!"
„Hast du also keine gekauft?"
„Ich habe nicht genug Geld dabeigehabt."
„Warum hast du mich nicht angerufen?"
„Ich habe deine Telefonnummer verloren!"

■ **3 Expressions of hope, fear, etc**
The subjunctive is also used in phrases such as:

Ich **hätte** gern ein neues Auto.	I would like a new car.
Ich dachte, du **kenntest** ihn schon.	I thought you already knew him.
Sie hoffte, ihre Freunde **würden** sie dort treffen.	She hoped her friends would meet her there.

■ **4 Als ob (as if)**

Sie tut, als ob sie die Chefin **sei**!	She acts as if she's the boss!
Er sah aus, als ob er ein Gespenst **gesehen hätte**.	He looked as if he'd seen a ghost.

■ 5 Wishes

Gott **sei** Dank!

Hätte ich nur das Geld!

Thank goodness!

If only I had the money!

▼ Modal verbs

Modal verbs are 'helping' verbs; rather than standing alone, they are added to other verbs to give a different meaning – they can express permission, ability, inclination, obligation, necessity and possibility. English examples are 'I **could** try that ...', 'He **must** have done it ...', 'You **mustn't** be late', 'She **ought** to be there'. They are most often used together with an infinitive and require no 'zu' before the infinitive.

▼ *Present tense (indicative)*

	Dürfen (may)	Können (can)	Mögen (like to)	Müssen (must)	Sollen (is to)	Wollen (want to)
ich	darf	kann	mag	muß	soll	will
du	darfst	kannst	magst	mußt	sollst	willst
er, sie, es	darf	kann	mag	muß	soll	will
Sie	dürfen	können	mögen	müssen	sollen	wollen
wir	dürfen	können	mögen	müssen	sollen	wollen
ihr	dürft	könnt	mögt	müßt	sollt	wollt
sie, Sie	dürfen	können	mögen	müssen	sollen	wollen

▼ *Present tense (subjunctive)*

	Dürfen	Können	Mögen	Müssen	Sollen	Wollen
ich	dürfe	könne	möge	müsse	solle	wolle
du	dürfest	könnest	mögest	müssest	sollest	wollest
er, sie, es	dürfe	könne	möge	müsse	solle	wolle
Sie	dürfen	können	mögen	müssen	sollen	wollen
wir	dürfen	können	mögen	müssen	sollen	wollen
ihr	dürfet	könnet	möget	müsset	sollet	wollet
sie, Sie	dürfen	können	mögen	müssen	sollen	wollen

▼ *The imperfect tense*

If you need to use a modal verb in the past, you can usually use the imperfect. These behave more or less like regular (weak) verbs (see page 53), except that all the umlauts disappear and the g in mögen changes to ch.

■ Indicative

	Dürfen	Können	Mögen	Müssen	Sollen	Wollen
ich	durfte	konnte	mochte	mußte	sollte	wollte
du	durftest	konntest	mochtest	mußtest	solltest	wolltest
er, sie, es	durfte	konnte	mochte	mußte	sollte	wollte
Sie	durften	konnten	mochten	mußten	sollten	wollten
wir	durften	konnten	mochten	mußten	sollten	wollten
ihr	durftet	konntet	mochtet	mußtet	solltet	wolltet
sie, Sie	durften	konnten	mochten	mußten	sollten	wollten

■ Subjunctive

	Dürfen	Können	Mögen	Müssen	Sollen	Wollen
ich	dürfte	könnte	möchte	müßte	sollte	wollte
du	dürftest	könntest	möchtest	müßtest	solltest	wolltest
er, sie, es	dürfte	könnte	möchte	müßte	sollte	wollte
Sie	dürften	könnten	möchten	müßten	sollten	wollten
wir	dürften	könnten	möchten	müßten	sollten	wollten
ihr	dürftet	könntet	möchtet	müßtet	solltet	wolltet
sie, Sie	dürften	könnten	möchten	müßten	sollten	wollten

▼ *The perfect and pluperfect tenses*

These tenses can be formed in one of two ways: either with the normal past participle (these don't have any umlauts – gekonnt, gewollt, etc.) or with the infinitive (können, wollen, etc.). If there's no infinitive in the sentence, use the normal past participle:

Ich habe es gewollt.   *I wanted it (to happen).*

If there is an infinitive already, use the infinitive of the modal verb:

Ich habe es tun wollen.   *I wanted to do it.*

The past participles are:

dürfen – gedurft
können – gekonnt
mögen – gemocht
müssen – gemußt
sollen – gesollt
wollen – gewollt

▼ *The future tense*
In the future tense, the modal infinitive goes to the end:

Er wird nicht kommen können.   *He won't be able to come.*

▼ *Modal verb checklist*
1. You don't need to put 'zu' before the infinitive.
2. The infinitive goes to the end.
3. Modal verbs are irregular in the singular of the present tense.
4. Dürfen, können, mögen and müssen don't have an umlaut in the imperfect indicative.
5. The subjunctive forms follow the weak verb pattern (see page 61).

▼ *Uses of modal verbs*
Below are some examples of the uses of individual verbs.

Dürfen

Ich darf nicht.	*I'm not allowed/may not.*
Er durfte alles machen.	*He was allowed to do anything.*
Es dürfte wahr sein.	*It might well be true.*

Können

Es kann sein.	*It may be.*
Es kann vielleicht regnen.	*It may rain.*
Er kann Deutsch.	*He knows German.*
Ich kann nichts dafür.	*I can't help it.*
Ich kann das unmöglich machen.	*I can't possibly do that.*
Er hat es tun können.	*He was able to do it. (ability)*
Er kann es getan haben.	*He might have done it. (possibility)*

Mögen

Er mag kommen.	*He may come.*
Das mag wohl sein.	*That may be.*
Ich möchte Deutschland besuchen.	*I would like to visit Germany.*

Müssen

Ich muß nicht.	*I don't have to. (contrast 'ich darf nicht' – I mustn't/am not allowed to)*
Ich mußte es tun.	*I had to do it.*
Er hat es tun müssen.	*He has had to do it. (obligation)*
Er muß es getan haben.	*He must have done it. (probability)*

Sollen

Was soll das sein?	*What is that supposed to be?*
Er soll reich sein.	*He's supposed to be rich.*
Was sollte ich anfangen?	*What was I to do?*
Ich sollte das machen.	*I ought to do that.*
Sie hätte es tun sollen.	*She ought to have done it.*
Sie soll es getan haben.	*She is supposed to have done it. (probability)*

Wollen

Ich will kommen.	*I want to come. (not 'I will come.')*
Wollen Sie mitkommen?	*Do you want to come with us?*
Ich will eben rausgehen.	*I'm just going out.*
Ich wollte eben rausgehen.	*I was just going out.*

▼ Activity 10   *Uses of modal verbs*

Fill in the gaps in the following conversation with
appropriate modal verbs in the correct tense.

„Guten Tag. ____ ich Ihnen ein paar Fragen stellen?"

„Na ja . . . Ich ____ um 2 wieder im Büro sein."

„Das ____ nur fünf Minuten dauern. ____ Sie sich hinsetzen?"

„Danke."

„Also . . . wußten Sie, daß die Farbe der Katzenfutterdose für die
Katze sehr wichtig ist?"

„Das ____ stimmen, aber wie ____ ich das wissen – ich habe keine
Katze."

„Aber Sie ____ zugeben, daß sich jedes Haustier für Dosen
interessiert."

„____ sein. Unser Hund ____ immer gefüttert werden."

„Sie haben einen Hund! Auch ihm wird unser neues Produkt
bestimmt schmecken."

„____ wohl sein – aber wie ____ ich das herausfinden?"

„Sie ____ einfach eine Dose mitnehmen. ____ Sie auch ein Formular
nehmen . . .?"

▼ Separable and inseparable verbs

A prefix – a few letters put on the front of a verb – can completely change the verb's meaning. Think about the English verbs **over**estimate, **under**estimate, **re**-estimate. The German verb 'steigen', meaning 'to climb', can become **ein**steigen (to get on or in), **aus**steigen (to get out of or off) or **um**steigen (to change [trains, etc]). The verb 'kommen' can also take a range of prefixes, but this time not all of the meanings are so similar: **an**kommen is to arrive, but **um**kommen is to die, and **ver**kommen is to rot or decline.

Some German prefixes are 'separable', some are 'inseparable' and some can be either. Separable prefixes move to the end of the sentence:

Ich **kam** in Berlin **an**.

whereas inseparable ones stay where they are:

Sie **bekam** ein Geschenk.

▼ *Inseparable prefixes*
These are:

be-	ent-	ge-	ver-
emp-	er-	miß-	and zer-

These prefixes stay on the front of the verb.

For example:

• verbringen *to spend time*
Er verbringt seine Ferien in Deutschland.

• zerbrechen *to break or shatter*
Sie zerbrach das Glas.

These verbs don't have a ge- in the past participle:

Er hat seine Ferien in Deutschland verbracht.
Sie hat das Glas zerbrochen.

In speech, the stress is always on the syllable following the prefix.

▼ *Separable or inseparable prefixes*

The most common are:

durch-	über-	unter-	wieder-
hinter-	um-	voll-	wider-

How do you tell if these prefixes are separable or inseparable? You could learn each verb as you come to it or you could check in your dictionary – you'll find the verbs listed as (sep.) or (insep.). You could listen for the stress (on the prefix if it's separable, on the next syllable if it's inseparable). However, there is also a rough rule you can apply.

If the verb expresses a physical action, it's separable. If it doesn't, it's inseparable. There are similar examples in English: contrast 'overcome' and 'come over'.

A German example is übersetzen. Über- means over and setzen to put. If we want to say 'the ferry took him across the river', that is exactly what the verb means, so it's separable:

Die Fähre **setzte** ihn über den Fluß **über.**

But übersetzen also means to translate and since this is not physically what the verb means, it's inseparable:

Er **übersetzte** den Brief.   *He translated the letter.*

Separable verbs do have a ge- in the past participle; it comes after the prefix. The past participle of übersetzen (inseparable) is **übersetzt.** The past participle of übersetzen (separable) is **übergesetzt.**

▼ *Separable prefixes*

Look at the first two lists. If the prefix isn't in those lists, then it's separable, e.g. fernsehen (to watch television), spazierengehen (to go for a walk), radfahren (to cycle).

Here is a checklist of points to remember:

1. The prefix comes off the front of the verb and goes to the end.

Ich **sehe** jeden Abend **fern.**
Er **geht** mit dem Hund **spazieren.**
Wir **fahren** am Wochenende **rad.**

2. In the past participle the ge- comes after the prefix:

Ich habe jeden Abend fern**ge**sehen.
Er ist mit dem Hund spazieren**ge**gangen.
Wir sind am Wochenende rad**ge**fahren.

3. If a separable verb is sent to the end (see word order, page 85), it all joins up again:

Wenn ich am Abend **fernsehe** . . .
Ich weiß, daß er gern **radfährt**.

4. If you use the infinitive of a separable verb with zu (see page 77), the zu comes after the prefix:

Er versuchte, aus dem Bus aus**zu**steigen.

5. The stress is on the prefix.

▼ **Activity 11** *Separable and inseparable verbs*

Complete the following passage, putting the verbs in brackets into the perfect or pluperfect tense. Are they separable or inseparable? There's a * if the verb takes sein.

Heute war ein katastrophaler Tag! Ich [verlassen] schon das Haus, dann [einfallen*] mir, daß ich den Mantel nicht [anziehen]. Der Bus [abfahren*] fast ohne mich, aber ich [einsteigen*] im letzten Augenblick. Dann [bemerken] ich, daß ich mir das Hemd [zerreißen]. Ich [sich zurückhalten], sofort auszusteigen; ich [weiterfahren], weil ich mit einem Kollegen [ausmachen], daß wir gemeinsam frühstücken würden. Es [mißlingen*] mir aber, ohne Schaden anzukommen: ich [vollstopfen] meine Tasche und sie dadurch [kaputtmachen]. Bücher, Papiere, Taschentücher . . . alles [hinausfallen*] beim Aussteigen!

▼ *Vocabulary*
es fällt mir ein *it occurs to me*
sich zurückhalten *to restrain yourself*
ausmachen *to arrange*
mißlingen *to fail (impersonal: see page 75)*

▼ Reflexive verbs

Reflexive verbs are a special type of verb used to indicate doing something related to yourself. We do have a few reflexive verbs in English – 'to behave yourself' is one example, 'to hurt yourself' is another. In German, many verbs are reflexive. In some cases it's easy to see why they are reflexive; for example, sich waschen (to get washed, to wash [yourself]). With others, it's less obvious: sich fühlen (to feel), sich vorstellen (to imagine).

Reflexive verbs are formed by adding a pronoun to the verb. This pronoun agrees with the subject. Except in the infinitive, the pronoun goes after the verb, just as the object does in 'Ich wasche das Auto'.

The pronouns are as follows:

To wash (yourself)

ich wasche **mich**	wir waschen **uns**
du wäschst **dich**	ihr wascht **euch**
er ⎱	sie waschen **sich**
sie ⎰ wäscht **sich**	Sie waschen **sich**
es	
Sie waschen **sich**	

The reflexive pronouns above are in the accusative because you use them when the person is the object of the action.

If you want to say 'I wash my hands' in German, you have to say 'I wash **to myself the** hands'. This time the pronoun is dative – it's 'die Hände' that goes into the accusative.

To wash your hands

ich wasche **mir** die Hände	wir waschen **uns** die Hände
du wäschst **dir** die Hände	ihr wascht **euch** die Hände
er ⎱	sie waschen **sich** die Hände
sie ⎰ wäscht **sich** die Hände	Sie waschen **sich** die Hände
es	
Sie waschen **sich** die Hände	

In these expressions the pronoun comes as soon after the subject as possible above. You **can** say, 'Er wäscht seine Hände' – but this means that the hands don't belong to the person doing the washing, but to someone else.

Reflexive verbs always form their perfect tense with 'haben'.

▼ The passive

The passive is used to describe the same event in a different way, often to give a different emphasis.

• *Active:* Der Hund **beißt** den Briefträger.   *The dog bites the postman.*

What does the biting? 'The dog'. Who gets bitten? 'The postman'.

• *Passive:* Der Briefträger **wird** von einem Hund **gebissen**.   *The postman is bitten by a dog.*

What does the biting? 'A dog'. Who gets bitten? 'The postman'.

Whether you use the active or passive depends on whom you're more interested in. The first sentence might be said by the dog's owner, the second by the village gossip! It's important to use what sounds natural – the passive is often used in more formal contexts, in newspaper reports and descriptions of procedures. Passive and active sentences are not really interchangeable. In speech the passive is often replaced, for example by 'man' (see page 32).

In the English passive phrase 'the postman is bitten', we use the verb 'to be' ('is') and a past participle ('bitten'). In German it's **werden**, not sein that's used.

Our example has the present passive. If you are talking about a past event (which is more likely in this case), your sentences would be:

Der Hund hat den Briefträger gebissen.
The dog has bitten the postman.
Der Briefträger **ist** von einem Hund **gebissen worden**.
The postman has been bitten by the dog.

In the perfect tense, the past participle goes to the end (as usual) and the passive sense is expressed with 'worden' (NB not 'geworden').

What else happens, when you make the change from active to passive? The subject in the active sentence still did the action but it comes after the word 'von' ('by') and is now called the 'agent'.

The other change is that the direct object becomes the subject, and so changes from accusative to nominative.

Here are another two examples:

Imperfect: Der Stein **zerbrach** das Fenster.
The stone broke the window.

Das Fenster **wurde** von dem Stein **zerbrochen**.
The window was broken by the stone.

Future: Der Vater **wird** die Kinder **abholen**.
The father will collect the children.

Die Kinder **werden** von ihrem Vater **abgeholt werden**.
The children will be collected by their father.

▼ *Avoiding the passive*

Sometimes you can get round using the passive, and it often sounds more natural. For example:

Niemand war zu sehen.	*Nobody was to be seen.*
Die Tür öffnete sich.	*The door was opened.*
Man machte das Fenster zu.	*The window was closed.*

If you are using a verb which takes the dative (see page 76), you have to use 'man' or turn the sentence round as follows:

Active: [Jemand] half ihm.
Passive: Man half ihm **or** Ihm wurde geholfen.

▼ *Is it really passive?*

In the passive something has to happen. Look at the example, 'the window was closed'. In English it's not clear if this is a **description** or an **action**. The German does make this clear.

Description: Das Fenster **war** geschlossen.
Action (and so passive): Das Fenster **wurde** geschlossen.

▼ Activity 12 *The passive*

Below is an eye-witness report of a crime. Make the underlined verbs passive. In each case, the object will become the subject.

Ein Junge <u>griff</u> unsere alte Nachbarin <u>an</u>. Die Polizei kam und <u>schleppte</u> ihn <u>weg</u>. Er <u>griff</u> ihre Handtasche und <u>schlug</u> sie ins Gesicht. Sie schrie sehr laut, aber ich glaube nicht, daß er sie schwer <u>verletzte</u>. Meine Frau <u>beruhigte</u> sie. Mein Sohn <u>hielt</u> den Verbrecher <u>fest</u>. Er ist erst 15, aber sehr kräftig! Dann <u>rief</u> ich die Polizei <u>an</u> und man <u>legte</u> dem Jungen Handschellen <u>an</u>. Entsetzlich, daß er so was am hellen Tag <u>versucht</u>!

▼ Impersonal verbs

Impersonal verbs always have the subject 'es'. A common German example is 'es gelang mir, das zu tun' – 'I succeeded in doing that' (literally 'it succeeded to me to do that').

The main impersonal verbs in German are:

• gefallen (to please, like)
Wie gefällt dir München?   *How do you like Munich?*

• gelingen (to succeed)
Es ist mir noch nicht gelungen,   *I haven't succeeded in reaching him*
ihn telefonisch zu erreichen.   *by telephone yet.*

• fehlen (to be lacking)
Fehlt dir etwas?   *Is anything wrong? (literally 'Are you lacking anything?')*

• schmecken (to taste good)
Das Essen hat gut geschmeckt.   *The food tasted good.*

Other useful impersonal phrases include:

es regnet, es schneit	*it's raining, it's snowing*
es gibt	*there is/are*
es klopft/klingelt	*someone's knocking/ringing the bell*
es tut mir leid	*I'm sorry*
es geht mir gut	*I'm well*
es ist mir warm/kalt	*I'm hot/cold*

es geht um (+ acc.)
es handelt sich um (+ acc.) } *it's about, it's a matter of*

es ist mir egal
es macht mir nichts aus } *I don't mind*

es lohnt sich *it's worth it*
es macht nichts *it doesn't matter*

▼ Activity 13 *Impersonal verbs*

Translate the following sentences into German, using an appropriate impersonal verb for each.

1. Did you manage to find the restaurant?
2. Yes – and the food was very good!
3. It was a long journey, but it was worth it.
4. It's about a poor German family.
5. I haven't got the courage [literally 'I'm lacking the courage'] to do that.
6. In that case I won't like it!
7. Are you cold? You can borrow my sweater.
8. I don't mind which film we see.

▼ Verbs that take the dative

The direct object is usually in the accusative case. However, there are several German verbs whose 'direct objects' go into the dative case.

Here is a list of the most common ones (see also the impersonal verbs on page 75):

antworten	*to answer (someone)*	glauben	*to believe (someone)*
begegnen	*to meet (by chance)*	gleichen	*to look like*
danken	*to thank*	gratulieren	*to congratulate*
drohen	*to threaten*	helfen	*to help*
erlauben	*to allow*	passen	*to suit*
folgen	*to follow*	passieren	*to happen*
gehorchen	*to obey*	raten	*to advise*
gehören	*to belong to*	verzeihen	*to forgive*
geschehen	*to happen (to someone)*	zuhören	*to listen to*
		zusehen	*to watch*

Some examples:

Ich begegnete **ihm** auf der Straße.	*I met him in the street.*
Ich bin einfach **der Menge** gefolgt.	*I simply followed the crowd.*
Sie helfen **ihrem Vater** im Garten.	*They're helping their father in the garden.*
Es ist **mir** schon oft passiert.	*It's happened to me a lot.*

▼ The infinitive and zu

An infinitive in English always includes the word 'to': 'I want **to go shopping**', 'they want **to buy** a computer'. In German you sometimes have to include the word 'zu' and sometimes you don't.

▼ *No zu*
- If you use a modal verb (see page 65):

Ich will fernsehen.	*I want to watch television.*
Sie möchten ins Kino gehen.	*They would like to go to the cinema.*

- With hören/sehen/lassen:

Ich hörte ihn singen.	*I heard him singing.*
Läßt du dir die Haare schneiden?	*Are you having your hair cut?*

▼ *With zu*
- All other verbs:

Es ist leicht, das zu sagen.	*That's easy to say.*
Es begann, heftig zu regnen.	*It began to rain heavily.*

- With um . . . zu to express purpose:

Ich fahre in Urlaub, um mich zu entspannen.	*I'm going on holiday to relax.*

▼ Forming commands (the imperative)

Imperatives let you give orders or make a request to a friend or a relative (the 'du' form), to more than one friend or relative (the 'ihr' form), or to a stranger (the 'Sie' form). Give orders to a stranger? Yes, you could be telling them how to get to the station!

▼ *The du-form*

This is formed in two ways:

(a) Take the stem of the verb and add -e. This -e is, however, often left out.

„Komm(e) hierher!"   *'Come here!'*
„Zeig(e) es mir!"   *'Show it to me!'*

(b) If the 'e' in the verb stem changes to 'i' or to 'ie' (see pages 99–102) then you just leave off the -st you add for the du form of the verb in the present tense.

„**Nimm** dir noch!" (du nimmst)   *'Take some more!'*
„**Sieh** dir das an!" (du siehst)   *'Look at that!'*

If you're using a separable verb or reflexive verb, the prefix or reflexive pronoun goes **to the end**. (The last example includes both!)

▼ *The ihr-form*

Take the ihr form of the present tense (see page 50) and leave out the ihr.

Ihr kommt mit – Kommt mit!   *Come with us!*
Ihr nehmt – Nehmt euch noch!   *Take some more!*

▼ *The Sie-form*

Take the Sie form of the present tense and turn it round.

Sie kommen – Kommen Sie mit!
Sie nehmen – Nehmen Sie sich noch!

▼ *Sein, haben and werden*

	Du	**Ihr**	**Sie**
Sein	sei!	seid!	seien Sie!
Haben	habe!	habt!	haben Sie!
Werden	wird!	werdet!	werden Sie!

▼ Activity 14 — *The imperative*

Put the verbs in the following sentences into the imperative.

1. [Aufstehen – du] – es ist schon nach acht!
2. [Sein – ihr] nicht so dumm!
3. [Geben – Sie] mir bitte ein Formular.
4. [Sich beeilen – ihr], sonst kommen wir zu spät.
5. [Kommen – Sie] bitte mit!
6. [Lesen – du] mir das vor!

▼ Replacing the English -ing form of the verb

There are several ways of replacing -ing:

1. You can use the **present participle** as an adjective, which is formed by adding -d on to the infinitive:

Eine lachen**de** Frau. *A laughing woman.*
Ein aufregen**des** Videospiel. *An exciting video game.*

The Germans only use this as **an adjective**, so it takes the usual endings.

2. You can use a **verbal noun**. Give the verb a capital letter and add 'das'.

Das Rauchen ist schädlich. *Smoking is harmful.*

3. How about 'the boy playing football'?
You could do this in two ways:

(a) der Fußball **spielende** Junge.

(b) der Junge, der Fußball spielt. *('the boy who is playing football')*
(See relative pronouns, page 36.)

(c) Then how about just using 'and'?

   Er saß da und las ein Buch.   *He sat there reading a book.*

(d) To express liking and preferring, you need the words 'gern'
   and 'lieber':

   Ich schwimme **gern**, aber ich jogge **lieber**.
   I like swimming but I prefer jogging.

(e) Don't get caught out by the English 'I am making' and
   'I was making'. These are simply present and past tenses,
   expressed by 'Ich mache' and 'Ich machte' in German.

▼ Activity 15   *Translating -ing forms*

Translate the following English sentences into German, using one
of the methods described above.

1. Swimming is very healthy.
2. She likes going to the theatre.
3. Did you see the child sleeping in the corner?
4. He's sitting in the kitchen eating soup.
5. Do you know the man playing the guitar?

▼ How long have you been . . .?

This is about the word '**seit**'. It means 'since', and the German
way of asking 'how long' is 'seit wann' – literally 'since when'.
This word 'seit' has an effect on the tense used in German, as
is shown by the examples below.

(a) How long have you been learning German? The perfect
tense in English. Seit wann **lernen** Sie Deutsch? The present.
Why? In German the idea is that you have been and **still are**

learning German. The English answer would be 'I have been learning German for two years'. The German answer 'Ich **lerne** Deutsch seit zwei Jahren'.
(b) When English uses the pluperfect 'had been . . .', in German you use the imperfect because you had been and **still were** . . .

He had been living in Berlin for two years when the wall came down.
Er **wohnte** seit zwei Jahren in Berlin, als die Mauer niedergerissen wurde.

He had been and he **still was living** there.
   If the sentence is negative, then the tense is the same in both languages:

Ich habe ihn seit Jahren nicht gesehen. *I haven't seen him for years.*

▼ Activity 16   *Seit*

Translate the following sentences into German, making sure that you use the correct tense with 'seit'.

1. We've lived in Manchester for four years.
2. How long have you worked in London?
3. He'd been waiting for an hour when the phone finally rang.
4. I haven't played tennis for years.
5. I'd wanted to see that film for ages ('seit langem').
6. How long had they known each other?

WORD ORDER
putting it all together

The order in which you can put the words in a German sentence is not as flexible as in English. There are certain rules which must be learnt, relating especially to where the verb should go in the sentence.

See also pages 26 and 30 for word order when using adverbs and pronouns.

▼ Verbs

(a) The **main verb** must be the **second piece of information** in a sentence unless you are asking a question (without a question word such as 'wo' or 'wann') or giving an order:

Sie **stehen** um sieben Uhr auf.

The first piece of information is the subject – Sie.

Um sieben Uhr **stehen** Sie auf.

The first piece of information is the time – um sieben Uhr.

Wenn es sieben Uhr ist, **stehen** Sie auf.

The first piece of information is the time – wenn es sieben Uhr ist.

But:

Stehen Sie um sieben Uhr auf! – an order.

Stehen Sie um sieben Uhr auf? – a question.

(b) Infinitives go to the end of the clause:

Wir werden nach Deutschland **fahren.**
Die Jungen wollen Fußball **spielen.**

(c) Past participles go to the end of the clause:

Wir sind nach Deutschland **gefahren.**
Die Jungen haben Fußball **gespielt.**

(d) Special rules apply after conjunctions. See page 83.

▼ Nicht

Nicht goes **as near to the end** of the sentence as possible:

Ich sehe ihn **nicht**.
Ich kann ihn **nicht** sehen (the infinitive must come last).
Ich habe ihn **nicht** gesehen (the past participle must come last).

However, you can change the order if you want to make one particular word negative:

Ich kann ihn **nicht** heute sehen.
I can't see him today (but I could see him tomorrow).

▼ Activity 1   *Jumbled sentences*

Put the words in the following sentences into the correct order.

1. Nach Spanien/jeden Sommer/Sie fahren/mit Ihrer Familie?
2. Wenn/im Garten/das Wetter/essen/ist schön/wir können.
3. Gehen/am Samstag/ich möchte/einkaufen.
4. Die gleiche Frage/gestellt/gerade/er hat.
5. Allein/nicht/gehen/ich will.
6. Nicht/ich wollte/den schwarzen Pulli/den blauen/sondern.

▼ Conjunctions

Conjunctions are words that join words or parts of a sentence (clauses) together:

Karl **und** sein Freund gingen zum Fußballspiel.
*Karl **and** his friend went to the football match.*

Die Eltern wohnten in einem Hotel, **aber** die Kinder schliefen in einem Zelt.
*The parents stayed in a hotel, **but** the children slept in a tent.*

Er war müde, **also** ging er ins Bett.
*He was tired **so** he went to bed.*

The 'joining word' can also come at the start of a sentence:

Als er in den Zug einstieg, fand er keinen Platz.
***When** he got on the train, he couldn't find a seat.*

Weil ich müde war, ging ich früh ins Bett.
Because I was tired, I went to bed early.

Conjunctions play a large part in word order by determining
where the verb goes. You may have noticed how the position
of the verb in the German sentences above varied according
to which conjunction was used. But, whichever you use, the
main verb is always the second piece of information. There are
three types of conjunction: co-ordinating, subordinating and
adverbial.

▼ (a) Co-ordinating conjunctions

These 'co-ordinate' or fit in with the rest of the sentence in
that they do not change the position of the verb. The chief
ones are:

aber	*but*
denn	*because*
oder	*or*
sondern	*but*
und	*and*

They link together parts of sentences that could stand alone:

Ich will ins Bett gehen. Ich bin müde.
Ich will ins Bett gehen, **denn** ich bin müde.
Er kaufte die Karten. Sie gingen ins Sportzentrum.
Er kaufte die Karten, **und** sie gingen ins Sportzentrum.

N.B. Use sondern rather than aber if all these conditions are
met:

• The first clause is negative.
• Both clauses have the same subject.
• The second clause contradicts the first. Contrast:

Er ist nicht reich, **sondern** arm.	*He's not rich, but poor.*
Er ist nicht reich, **aber** glücklich.	*He's not rich, but he's happy.*

There are also a few **pairs** of conjunctions:

entweder/oder	*either/or*
nicht nur/sondern auch	*not only/but also*
weder/noch	*neither/nor*

Entweder werde ich nach Italien fahren, **oder** ich werde zu Hause
bleiben und Geld sparen.
I'll either go to Italy or stay at home and save money.

▼ *(b) Subordinating conjunctions*

After a subordinating conjunction, the verb goes to the end:

Machen wir einen Spaziergang, **bevor** es zu regnen **anfängt?**
Shall we go for a walk before it starts to rain?

If the subordinate clause comes first, it is immediately followed by the main verb and the subject has to come **second**:

Subordinating conjunction	Verb to end	'Inversion' of subject and verb

Weil es kalt **war, trug** er ein Paar Handschuhe.
Because it was cold, he wore a pair of gloves.

Als der Zug **ankam, wartete** er schon auf dem Bahnsteig.
When the train arrived, he was already waiting on the platform.

In this kind of sentence, the two clauses could not exist on their own.

The main subordinating conjunctions are:

als	*when, as*	seitdem	*since (time)*
bevor	*before*	so daß	*so that*
bis	*until*	während	*while*
da	*since, because*	warum	*why*
damit	*so that*	weil	*because*
daß	*that*	wenn	*when*
nachdem	*after*	wie	*how*
ob	*whether*	wo	*where*
obwohl	*although*		

■ So daß or damit?

Both of these mean 'so that'. However, there is a difference! 'So daß' is used in **result** clauses:

Sie machte das Fenster auf, **so daß** ich fror.
She opened the window, so that [with the result that] I was freezing.

'Damit' is used in **purpose** clauses:

Sie machte das Fenster auf, **damit** wir alle aufwachen würden.
She opened the window, so that [with the intention that] we would all wake up.

■ **Als or wenn?**

These both mean 'when': 'als' when talking about the past, and 'wenn' when describing the present or the future, but also when talking about events that occurred more than once in the past.

Als ich ein Kind war, schmeckte mir Spinat nicht.
When I was a child, I didn't like spinach.

Wenn ich Spinat sehe, wird's mir übel.
Whenever I see spinach, I feel sick.

Wenn ich Spinat bekam, beschwerte ich mich heftig.
Whenever I was given spinach, I complained heartily.

▼ *(c) Adverbial conjunctions*

These are so-called because they 'add' some information to the verb. They are followed immediately by the verb. The main ones are:

also	*so, therefore*
auch	*also*
außerdem	*besides, moreover*
daher, darum	*so, therefore*
dann	*then*
deshalb, deswegen	*therefore, for that reason*
inzwischen	*meanwhile*
jedoch	*yet, nevertheless*
kaum	*hardly, scarcely*
sonst	*or else, otherwise*
trotzdem	*in spite of that*
übrigens	*by the way, incidentally*
und zwar	*and in fact*

Examples:

Es regnete, **also** blieben wir zu Hause.
It was raining, so we stayed at home.

Beeil' dich, **sonst** verpassen wir den Zug.
Hurry up, or we'll miss the train.

Das Buch war ziemlich teuer, **trotzdem** habe ich es gekauft.
The book was quite expensive, but I bought it anyway.

▼ Activity 2   *Conjunctions*

Join each pair of clauses using one of the conjunctions in the box. Change the word order where necessary.

1. Anna war am Tisch sehr still/sie war sonst sehr gesprächig.
2. Ihre Mutter wußte sofort/etwas war mit ihr los.
3. Sie wartete/sie war mit dem Essen fertig.
4. Sie sprach mit ihr/sie räumten zusammen den Tisch ab.
5. Sie erfuhr/sie hatte so wenig gesagt.
6. Anna hatte Angst/mehrere ihrer Arbeitskollegen waren entlassen worden.
7. Sie fragte sich/ihre Stellung wäre sicher.
8. Ihre Mutter beruhigte sie/sie machte sich Sorgen um ihre Tochter.

as	although	why	whether
until	in spite of that	that	because

▼▼▼
FURTHER USEFUL
INFORMATION

▼ Some notes on punctuation

The examples below show some of the main ways in which English and German punctuation differ. The most important difference is probably the use of the comma: there are certain instances in German where it's not a matter of choice as to whether you use one or not!

▼ *The comma*

In German you must use a comma

(a) If the subject of a sentence is changed or repeated:

Er arbeitet im Garten, und sie sitzt im Wohnzimmer.
Er sagte, er wollte in die Stadt gehen.

(b) Before a subordinating or an adverbial conjunction:

Ich wußte, daß ich den Zug verpaßt hatte.
Er war müde, also ging er ins Bett.

(c) Before zu + infinitive if there is something else in the clause:

Es begann zu regnen.
Es begann, heftig zu regnen.

N.B. There is a full stop rather than a comma after the thousands in numbers:

3.000   1.000.000.

In German the comma is used instead of the decimal point: 2,6 (and is included in speech: „zwei komma sechs").

▼ *The colon*

The colon is used to introduce direct speech:

Er sagte: „Der Zug fährt in zehn Minuten ab."

▼ *The full stop*
If this is used in abbreviations, you should say the actual words:

z.B. zum Beispiel
d.h. das heißt

If there is no full stop in the abbreviation, you just say the letters:

Pkw (Personalkraftwagen), USA

A full stop after a number shows that it is an ordinal number (see page 91): der 1. = der erste (the 1st), der 4. = der vierte (the 4th).

▼ *Inverted commas/speech marks*
German speech marks are as below:

Er fragte: „Wollen wir ins Kino gehen?"

▼ Numbers, times and dates
We use two types of numbers – **cardinal** (one, two, three, etc.) and **ordinal**, which tell you the order things come in (first, second, third, etc.).

▼ *Cardinal numbers*
1–90

0 null	11 elf
1 eins	12 zwölf
2 zwei	13 dreizehn
3 drei	14 vierzehn
4 vier	15 fünfzehn
5 fünf	16 sechzehn (NB 'sechs' loses the 's')
6 sechs	17 siebzehn (NB 'sieben' loses the 'en')
7 sieben	18 achtzehn
8 acht	19 neunzehn
9 neun	20 zwanzig
10 zehn	

After 20, the single numbers are added on as follows:

21 einundzwanzig (NB no 's' on 'eins')
22 zweiundzwanzig, etc.

30 dreißig (NB ß not z)
40 vierzig
50 fünfzig
60 sechzig (again no 's')
70 siebzig (again no 'en')
80 achtzig
90 neunzig

▼ Activity 1 *Numbers*

Can you write out the following numbers in words?

1. 22		**6.** 77
2. 33		**7.** 88
3. 44		**8.** 99
4. 55		**9.** 23
5. 66		**10.** 32

■ 100 and over

100 is (ein) hundert. You don't usually need the 'ein'.
Remember that it ends in **-ert**, unlike the English **-red.**
200 is zweihundert, and so on.
201 is zweihunderteins – all one word.
222 is zweihundertzweiundzwanzig – again all one word.

Of course you would write these in figures, but you need to know how to say them.

▼ Activity 2 *Numbers over 100*

How would you write out these numbers?

1. 345
2. 578
3. 999
4. 666
5. 721

■ Thousands and millions . . .

1.000 is tausend.
2.000 is zweitausend.
Remember that it ends in -end, unlike the English -and.
So 2,200 in English is 2.200 in German and would be written
as zweitausendzweihundert. (See page 88 for the use of full
stops and commas with numbers.)
1.000.000 is eine Million.
2.000.000 is zwei Millionen.

▼ Ordinal numbers

'The first snow', 'the tenth commandment': remember that
these are adjectives (see page 14). You form them as follows:

■ 1–19

Add -**te** to the cardinal number:

zwei – zweite, vier – vierte.

But there are some exceptions, as there are in English (first,
third):

eins – erste;
drei – dritte;
sieben – siebte *(or, less often,* siebente*)*;
acht – achte *(only one t: compare English eight and eighth).*

■ 20–100

Add -**ste** to the cardinal number:

zwanzig – zwanzigste;
zweiundzwanzig – zweiundzwanzigste;
dreißig – dreißigste.

■ 101 and over

Just start all over again:

hunderteins – hunderterste;
hundertzwei – hundertzweite.

When we write these figures in English, we use the
abbreviations **1st**, **2nd**, **3rd**, **4th**, and so on. In German
you just put a full stop after the number: 1., 2., 3., 4.

▼ *Other uses of numbers*

■ Fractions

Just put -l on the end of the ordinal number:

⅓ ein Drittel
¼ ein Viertel (note that these are nouns with capital letters).

Eine Viertelstunde (quarter of an hour) is all one word.

■ Half?

'Half' is 'halb' or 'die Hälfte', depending on what you mean:
Half **a** bottle is eine **halbe** Flasche.
Half **the** bottle (when you mean a particular one) is **die Hälfte** der Flasche.
1½ can be eineinhalb or anderthalb.
2½ is zweieinhalb.
3½ is dreieinhalb.

■ To multiply . . .

Add -**mal** ('times'):

Zweimal zwei ist vier.   *Two times two is four.*
Ich habe es zweimal gemacht.   *I've done it twice.*

■ Firstly, etc.

Put -**ns** on the end of the ordinal number:
Erstens is firstly, zweitens is secondly, and so on.

■ Approximately

The German words for 'about' or 'approximately' are ungefähr and circa:

Er ist ungefähr eine Viertelstunde später gekommen.
He came about quarter of an hour later.

Die Temperatur ist circa dreißig Grad.
The temperature is about thirty degrees.

■ Telephone numbers

The Germans often use the word 'zwo' instead of 'zwei' on the telephone, so that it is not confused with the similar-sounding 'drei'. It is also worth noting that German telephone numbers are given in pairs of digits, so 69 32 21 would be 'neunundsechzig, zweiunddreißig, einundzwanzig'.

▼ Times

There are several ways of **asking** the time in German:

Wie spät ist es?
Wieviel Uhr ist es?
Wieviel Uhr haben wir?

As in English, there are several ways of **telling** the time:

9.00	neun Uhr
9.05	neun Uhr fünf
	fünf nach neun
	fünf Minuten nach neun
3.50	drei Uhr fünfzig
	zehn vor vier
	zehn Minuten vor vier

You need to remember that 'past' is **nach** and 'to' is **vor**.

▼ Activity 3   *Times*

How could you say these times?

1. 2.10
2. 4.20
3. 6.50
4. 8.12
5. 9.36

Expressing other times is slightly more complicated. For 'quarter past', the Germans also use 'quarter **to the next hour**', so:

9.15   could be 'neun Uhr fünfzehn' or 'Viertel nach neun' but also 'viertel zehn' (quarter of the way to ten).
        This is actually more common in everyday speech. As in English, 'neun Uhr fünfzig', etc. is used more for train times, arrangements, etc.

9.30   could be 'neun Uhr dreißig' but also 'halb zehn' (half of the way to ten). Don't worry if it takes a while to get used to the fact that 'halb zehn' does **not** mean half past ten!

9.45   could be 'neun Uhr fünfundvierzig', etc. but also 'dreiviertel zehn' (three-quarters of the way to ten).

The Germans also talk about 'five to half past' and 'six past half past'.

▼ Activity 4 *More times*

Write these times in numbers.

1. Halb elf
2. Viertel sieben
3. Halb sechs
4. Dreiviertel fünf
5. Sechs Uhr fünfzehn
6. Vier vor halb eins
7. Drei nach halb vier

■ A.m. and p.m.

12 noon is Mittag or zwölf Uhr.
12 midnight is Mitternacht or vierundzwanzig Uhr.
The Germans use the 24-hour clock more than the British, so
2.20 p.m. is vierzehn Uhr zwanzig. Otherwise:

a.m. is morgens or vormittags ('morgens' being roughly the
      time up to 9 a.m.).
p.m. is nachmittags (afternoon) or abends (evening).

Use nachts for night-time and the early hours of the morning.

■ At and about?

Um ein Uhr	*At one o'clock*
Um halb neun	*At half-past eight*
Gegen ein Uhr	} *At about one o'clock*
Etwa um ein Uhr	

■ At what time of day?

Am Tag	*During the daytime*
Am Morgen *or* morgens	*In the morning*
(NB no capital 'm')	
Am Nachmittag *or* nachmittags	*In the afternoon*
Am Abend *or* abends	*In the evening*
In der Nacht *or* nachts	*At night*

See also prepositions, page 43.

▼ Days and dates

Montag	*Monday*
Dienstag	*Tuesday*
Mittwoch	*Wednesday*
Donnerstag	*Thursday*
Freitag	*Friday*
Samstag/Sonnabend	*Saturday*
Sonntag	*Sunday*

'Samstag' is used in the south of Germany and Austria, whereas 'Sonnabend' is used in the north of Germany.

The months are as follows:

Januar (Jänner *in Austria*)	*January*
Februar	*February*
März	*March*
April	*April*
Mai	*May*
Juni	*June*
Juli	*July*
August	*August*
September	*September*
Oktober	*October*
November	*November*
Dezember	*December*

■ How to ask what the date is
There are several ways in German:

Der wievielte ist es heute?
Welches Datum haben wir heute?
Den wievielten haben wir heute?

■ How to say what the date is
Just as in English, you use ordinal numbers (see page 91). But ordinal numbers are adjectives, so if you write the date out in full, you need to use the correct case and ending (see page 9):

Heute ist **der** erste Januar.
Heute haben wir **den** ersten Januar.

If you don't write it out in full, just put a **full stop** after the number:

Heute ist der **1.** Januar.
Heute haben wir den **1.** Januar.

■ Prepositions with days and dates

Am Montag   *On Monday*
Im Januar   *In January*

Notice the use of the definite article; the same goes for all the days, months and seasons:

Im Frühling   *In spring*
Im Sommer   *In summer*
Im Herbst   *In autumn*
Im Winter   *In winter*

■ Years

In 1066 is either '1066' (no word for 'in') or 'im Jahre 1066' – **never** 'in 1066'. 1816 is said as 'achtzehn**hundert**sechzehn' and never as 'achtzehnsechzehn'.

■ Today, etc.

heute	*today*
gestern	*yesterday*
morgen	*tomorrow*
vorgestern	*the day before yesterday*
übermorgen	*the day after tomorrow*
heute morgen	*this morning*
gestern abend	*last night*
morgen früh	*tomorrow morning*

IRREGULAR VERBS

▼▼▼
IRREGULAR VERBS

Infinitive	present (if irregular)	Imperfect (and subjunctive)	Past participle (*= sein)
BACKEN *bake*		backte	gebacken
BEFEHLEN *command*	befiehlt	befahl (beföhle)	befohlen
BEGINNEN *begin*		begann	begonnen
BEIßEN *bite*		biß	gebissen
BIEGEN *bend*		bog	gebogen
BIETEN *offer*		bot	geboten
BINDEN *tie*		band	gebunden
BITTEN *ask*		bat	gebeten
BLASEN *blow*	bläst	blies	geblasen
BLEIBEN *stay*		blieb	*geblieben
BRATEN *roast*	brät	briet	gebraten
BRECHEN *break*	bricht	brach	*gebrochen
BRENNEN *burn*		brannte (brennte)	gebrannt
BRINGEN *bring*		brachte	gebracht
DENKEN *think*		dachte	gedacht
DRINGEN *be urgent*		drang	gedrungen
DÜRFEN *be allowed*	ich/er darf	durfte	gedurft/dürfen
EMPFEHLEN *recommend*	empfiehlt	empfahl (empföhle)	empfohlen
ERLÖSCHEN *die out*	erlischt	erlosch	*erloschen
ERSCHRECKEN *be startled*	erschrickt	erschrak	*erschrocken
ESSEN *eat*	ißt	aß	gegessen
FAHREN *travel*	fährt	fuhr	*gefahren
FALLEN *fall*	fällt	fiel	*gefallen
FANGEN *catch*	fängt	fing	gefangen
FINDEN *find*		fand	gefunden
FLIEGEN *fly*		flog	*geflogen
FLIEHEN *flee*		floh	*geflohen
FLIEßEN *flow*		floß	*geflossen
FRESSEN *eat (of animals)*	frißt	fraß	gefressen
FRIEREN *freeze*		fror	*gefroren
GEBÄREN *bear (child)*	gebärt, gebiert	gebar	geboren
GEBEN *give*	gibt	gab	gegeben
GEHEN *go*		ging	*gegangen
GELINGEN *succeed*		gelang	*gelungen
GELTEN *be valid*	gilt	galt (gölte)	gegolten
GENESEN *recover*		genas	*genesen
GENIEßEN *enjoy*		genoß	genossen
GESCHEHEN *happen*	geschieht	geschah	*geschehen
GEWINNEN *win*		gewann (gewönne)	gewonnen

GIEßEN *pour*		goß	gegossen
GLEICHEN *resemble*		glich	geglichen
GLEITEN *slip*		glitt	*geglitten
GRABEN *dig*	gräbt	grub	gegraben
GREIFEN *grasp*		griff	gegriffen
HABEN *have*	du hast; er hat	hatte	gehabt
HALTEN *hold*	hält	hielt	gehalten
HÄNGEN *hang*		hing	gehangen
HEBEN *raise*		hob	gehoben
HEIßEN *be called*		hieß	geheißen
HELFEN *help*	hilft	half (hülfe)	geholfen
KENNEN *know*		kannte (kennte)	gekannt
KLINGEN *sound*		klang	geklungen
KOMMEN *come*		kam	*gekommen
KÖNNEN *can*	ich/er kann	konnte	gekonnt/können
KRIECHEN *crawl*		kroch	*gekrochen
LADEN *load*	lädt	lud	geladen
LASSEN *let*	läßt	ließ	gelassen/lassen
LAUFEN *run*	läuft	lief	*gelaufen
LEIDEN *suffer*		litt	gelitten
LEIHEN *lend*		lieh	geliehen
LESEN *read*	liest	las	gelesen
LIEGEN *lie*		lag	gelegen
LÜGEN *tell lies*		log	gelogen
MESSEN *measure*	mißt	maß	gemessen
MIßLINGEN *fail*		mißlang	*mißlungen
MÖGEN *like*	ich/er mag	mochte	gemocht/mögen
MÜSSEN *must*	ich/er muß	mußte	gemußt/müssen
NEHMEN *take*	nimmt	nahm	genommen
NENNEN *name*		nannte (nennte)	genannt
PFEIFEN *whistle*		pfiff	gepfiffen
RATEN *advise*	rät	riet	geraten
REIBEN *rub*		rieb	gerieben
REIßEN *tear*		riß	gerissen
REITEN *ride*		ritt	*geritten
RENNEN *run*		rannte (rennte)	*gerannt
RIECHEN *smell*		roch	gerochen
RUFEN *call*		rief	gerufen
SCHAFFEN *create/manage*		schuf	geschaffen
SCHEIDEN *separate*		schied	*geschieden
SCHEINEN *seem*		schien	geschienen
SCHELTEN *scold*	schilt	schalt (schölte)	gescholten
SCHIEBEN *push*		schob	geschoben
SCHIEßEN *shoot*		schoß	geschossen
SCHLAFEN *sleep*	schläft	schlief	geschlafen
SCHLAGEN *hit*	schlägt	schlug	geschlagen

SCHLEICHEN *creep*		schlich	*geschlichen
SCHLIEßEN *shut*		schloß	geschlossen
SCHMEIßEN *fling*		schmiß	geschmissen
SCHMELZEN *melt*	schmilzt	schmolz	*geschmolzen
SCHNEIDEN *cut*		schnitt	geschnitten
SCHREIBEN *write*		schrieb	geschrieben
SCHREIEN *shout*		schrie	geschrie(e)n
SCHREITEN *step*		schritt	*geschritten
SCHWEIGEN *be silent*		schwieg	geschwiegen
SCHWELLEN *swell*	schwillt	schwoll	*geschwollen
SCHWIMMEN *swim*		schwamm (schwömme)	*geschwommen
SCHWÖREN *swear*		schwur (schwüre)	geschworen
SEHEN *see*	sieht	sah	gesehen
SEIN *be*	ich bin; du bist; er ist; wir/sie sind; ihr seid	war	*gewesen
SENDEN *send, broadcast*		sandte/sendete	gesandt
SINGEN *sing*		sang	gesungen
SINKEN *sink*		sank	*gesunken
SITZEN *sit*		saß	gesessen
SOLLEN *is to*	ich/er soll	sollte	gesollt/sollen
SPRECHEN *speak*	spricht	sprach	gesprochen
SPRINGEN *jump*		sprang	*gesprungen
STECHEN *stab*	sticht	stach	gestochen
STEHEN *stand*		stand (stünde)	gestanden
STEHLEN *steal*	stiehlt	stahl	gestohlen
STEIGEN *climb*		stieg	*gestiegen
STERBEN *die*	stirbt	starb (stürbe)	*gestorben
STINKEN *stink*		stank	gestunken
STOßEN *push*	stößt	stieß	gestoßen
STREICHEN *stroke*		strich	gestrichen
STREITEN *quarrel*		stritt	gestritten
TRAGEN *carry*	trägt	trug	getragen
TREFFEN *meet*	trifft	traf	getroffen
TREIBEN *drive*		trieb	getrieben
TRETEN *step*	tritt	trat	*getreten
TRINKEN *drink*		trank	getrunken
TRÜGEN *deceive*		trog	getrogen
TUN *do*	ich tue; du tust er/ihr tut; wir/sie tun	tat	getan
VERBERGEN *hide*	verbirgt	verbarg	verborgen
VERDERBEN *spoil*	verdirbt	verdarb (verdürbe)	verdorben
VERGESSEN *forget*	vergißt	vergaß	vergessen
VERLIEREN *lose*		verlor	verloren
VERMEIDEN *avoid*		vermied	vermieden
VERSCHWINDEN *disappear*		verschwand	*verschwunden
VERZEIHEN *excuse*		verzieh	verziehen
WACHSEN *grow*	wächst	wuchs	*gewachsen
WASCHEN *wash*	wäscht	wusch	gewaschen
WEISEN *point*		wies	gewiesen

WENDEN *turn*		wandte (wendete)	gewandt
WERBEN *advertise*	wirbt	warb (würbe)	geworben
WERDEN *become*	du wirst; er wird	wurde	*geworden/ worden
WERFEN *throw*	wirft	warf (würfe)	geworfen
WIEGEN *weigh/rock*		wog/wiegte	gewogen
WISSEN *know*	ich/er weiß	wußte	gewußt
WOLLEN *want*	ich/er will	wollte	gewollt/wollen
ZIEHEN *pull*		zog	gezogen
ZWINGEN *force*		zwang	gezwungen

ANSWERS
TO ACTIVITIES

▼▼▼
ANSWERS
TO ACTIVITIES

▼ Nouns

Activity 1
(1) (b) eine (2) (a) der (3) (a) am or an dem (4) (a) die
(5) (c) kein (6) (a) zum or zu dem (7) (b) ein (8) (a) den
(9) (c) no article (10) (c) no article (11) (a) den
(12) (c) kein.

Activity 2
1. die 2. das 3. das 4. der 5. die 6. das 7. die 8. der.

Activity 3
1. Hände 2. Colas 3. Wohnungen 4. Autos, Fahrräder,
Straßen 5. Bilder 6. Blumen 7. Fenster 8. Mannschaften.

Activity 4
(1) Nom (2) Gen (3) Nom (4) Dat (5) Acc (6) Acc
(7) Acc (8) Acc (9) Nom (10) Gen (11) Acc (12) Dat
(13) Acc (14) Acc (15) Acc (16) Acc (17) Dat (18) Gen
(19) Acc (20) Acc (21) Dat (22) Acc.

Activity 5
(Acc) den Hund, (Acc) einen Knochen, (Dat) den Kindern,
(Acc) ein Wurstbrot, (Acc) eine Gurke, (Acc) ein Brot, (Acc)
den Vater, (Acc) das Auto, (Gen) seines Kollegen, (Acc) seinen
Namen, (Acc) den Nachbarn, (Acc) die Fotos, (Gen) seiner
Frau, (Dat) am Montag, (Acc) keine Zeit.

▼ Adjectives

Activity 1
Der <u>neue</u> Roman von Waltraud Anna Mitgutsch . . .
. . . ist die Geschichte einer <u>jungen</u> Frau, deren Kind <u>autistisch</u>
ist. Das Buch ist <u>erschütternd</u> und oft <u>traurig</u>. Es ist aber auch
eine <u>tolle</u> Liebesgeschichte zwischen Mutter und Kind. Die
<u>österreichische</u> Schriftstellerin hat schon wieder eine <u>spannende</u>
Erzählung geschrieben.

Activity 2

wunderschöne, kleinen, hohe, blaue, schottische, dick, guten, seltsames, freundlich, naheliegenden, gemütliches, interessanten.

Activity 3

1. gute 2. schwarzen 3. derselben 4. Süßes 5. aller, dieser.

Activity 4

(1) diesem (2) diese (3) diesem (4) diese (5) Diese.

Activity 5

1. kälter, am kältesten 2. schneller, am schnellsten 3. dunkler, am dunkelsten 4. härter, am härtesten.

Activity 6

das beste, teurer als, einen dümmeren, den exklusivsten, so klar wie, einen besseren Geruch als, weniger langweilig, die saubersten.

Activity 7

1. Verwandten 2. Bekannten 3. Deutschen 4. Fremder.

Activity 8

Deinen, Deiner, ihr, unseren, meinem, seinen, meiner.

▼ Adverbs

Activity 1

immer, gut, stundenlang, nachts, süß, sofort, morgens, sehr effektiv, schnell, klar, sorgenfreier.

Activity 2

1. Ich gehe oft zu Fuß ins Sportzentrum.
2. Im Sommer liegt die Katze stundenlang im Garten.
3. Manchmal frühstücken wir auf dem Balkon/Wir frühstücken manchmal auf dem Balkon.
4. Bist du letztes Jahr mit dem Zug nach Österreich gefahren?
5. Wir treffen uns heute um 4 Uhr in dem Café.

Activity 3

leiser, lauter, lieber, früher, weniger aggressiv, höflicher, am öftesten, vernünftiger, besser.

▼ Pronouns

Activity 1
„Hallo Gabi! Hier ist die Karin. Ich (per) gehe heute abend ins Kino. Kommst du (per) mit? Oder hast du (per) schon etwas (indef) vor?"
„Eigentlich nichts (neg) Besonderes. Was (interrog) siehst du (per) dir (refl) an? Wahrscheinlich etwas (indef) Verrücktes."
„Überhaupt nicht. Ich (per) habe den Titel des Filmes vergessen, aber er (per) geht um einen großen Liebhaber."
„Ah ja? Und wer (interrog) spielt ihn (per)?"
„Niemand (neg), den (rel) ich (per) kenne."
„Also warum interessierst du (per) dich (refl) dafür (per)?"
„Jemand (indef) hat mir (per) davon (per) erzählt . . . Peter, der (demons) hat ihn (per) gesehen."
„Okay. Soll ich (per) dich (per) abholen? Fahren wir (per) mit meinem Auto?"
„Nein, nehmen wir (per) lieber meines (pos). Man (indef) weiß nie, ob man (indef) eine Fahrt mit dir (per) überleben wird!"
„Das (demons) ist aber eine Frechheit!"

Activity 2
1. Sie ist in die Stadt gefahren.
2. Sie schenkt es ihr.
3. Ich mag ihn nicht.
4. Ich werde sie ihm erzählen.
5. Hast du sie ihnen gegeben?
6. Ich habe sie irgendwo gesehen.

Activity 3
etwas, keines, jemand, einer, Jemand, keiner/niemand, etwas, man, etwas, einem, etwas.

Activity 4
1. wen 2. unseres 3. deiner 4. wessen 5. welches/was für ein 6. welchen/was für einen 7. deines 8. wem; mir/deiner.

Activity 5 (possible answers)
1. **Warum** fährt er nach Deutschland? **Wo** fährt er hin? **Wen** besucht er? In **welche** Stadt fährt er? **Wie** fährt er nach Deutschland? Mit **wem** fährt er? **Wohin** fährt er? **Wann** genau fährt er? **Was** macht er dort?

2. **Wo** war die Party? **Was** habt ihr gemacht? **Wie** war das Essen? **Was** habt ihr getrunken? **Wen** habt ihr getroffen? **Was** gab es zu essen? **Welche** Musik habt ihr gehört? **Wer** war da? **Was** habt ihr mitgebracht? **Wann** seid ihr heimgekommen? **Wie** seid ihr heimgekommen?

3. **Welches** Buch hat sie gekauft? **Wo** hat sie es gekauft? **Was** hat es gekostet? **Worum** geht es in dem Buch? **Wann** liest sie es? **Wem** schenkt sie es? Vom **welchem** Verlag ist es herausgegeben? **Warum** braucht sie es?

4. **Welchen** Film willst du sehen? In **welchem** Kino läuft er? **Worum** geht er? **Wer** spielt mit? **Wer** ist der Regisseur? **Wieviel** kostet das Kino? **Wann** gehst du? Mit **wem** gehst du? **Was** machst du danach? **Wie** heißt er? **Wo** läuft er?

Activity 6
1. Ich kenne eine interessante Frau, **die** Wissenschaftlerin ist.
2. Hast du mit dem Mann gesprochen, **dessen** Sohn in Deutschland arbeitet?
3. Ich habe am Wochenende Tennis gespielt, **was** mir immer Spaß macht.
4. Wir haben in Hotels übernachtet, **die** ganz billig waren.
5. Alles, **was** er gesagt hat, war interessant/Er hat viel gesagt, **was** interessant war.
6. Sie spielen ein Lied, **das** mir sehr gut gefällt.
7. Ich fahre mit dem Zug, **der** immer Verspätung hat./Der Zug, mit **dem** ich fahre, hat immer Verspätung.
8. Willst du das Buch lesen, von **dem/wovon** ich dir erzählt habe?

▼ Prepositions

Activity 1
„Meine Damen und Herren, <u>in</u> (dat) wenigen Minuten werden wir <u>in</u> (dat) Heathrow landen. <u>Wegen</u> (gen) der starken Winde <u>während</u> (gen) des Flugs haben wir leider eine kleine Verspätung. Bitte kehren Sie <u>zu</u> (dat) Ihrem Platz zurück und schnallen Sie sich an. Stellen Sie ihr Handgepäck <u>unter</u> (acc) den Sitz <u>vor</u> (dat) Ihnen. Achten Sie bitte darauf, daß Ihr Sitz aufrecht ist und daß der Tisch <u>vor</u> (dat) Ihnen hochgeklappt ist.

<u>Von</u> (dat) der linken Seite des Flugzeugs können Sie Big Ben und die Houses of Parliament sehen. Das Wetter <u>in</u> (dat)

London ist sonnig. Es hat <u>über</u> (dat) zwanzig Grad. Die Ortszeit ist fünf Minuten <u>nach</u> (dat) vier.
   <u>Im</u> (dat) Namen <u>von</u> (dat) Flugkapitän Smith und seiner Besatzung möchte ich Ihnen einen angenehmen Aufenthalt <u>in</u> (dat) England wünschen und mich <u>bei</u> (dat) Ihnen bedanken, daß Sie unsere Fluglinie gewählt haben."

Activity 2
in den (acc), in eine andere (acc), in dem/im (dat), auf den (acc), neben die Gläser (acc), hinter dem (dat), unter das (acc), vor den Gästen (dat).

Activity 3
1. Möchtest du an einer Schauspielproduktion teilnehmen? (dat)
2. Sie haben mir bei dem Abwaschen geholfen. (dat)
3. Wir haben vor einigen Tagen ein neues Auto gekauft. (dat)
4. Viele Passagiere beklagten sich über die Verspätung. (acc)
5. Interessierst du dich für Fußball? (acc)
6. Als er an die Reihe kam/war, kaufte er eine Fahrkarte nach Berlin. (acc, dat)
7. Ich kaufte zwei CDs zu £10.99 das Stück. (acc)
8. Er parkte sein Auto in der Nähe des Bahnhofs/nahe am Bahnhof. (dat)
9. Meiner Meinung nach sollte der Minister zurücktreten. (dat)
10. Sie ist so stolz auf sich! (acc)

▼ Verbs

Activity 1
Waagerecht
1. mischen   3. sucht   4. nähe   5. tun   7. trinke   9. füllt
10. stehen.

Senkrecht
1. machst   2. schade   3. senden   4. nennt   6. geht   8. rufst.

Activity 2
bist, denkst, kommst, liest, hilfst, wäschst, machst, siehst, fährst, trinkst.

Activity 3
war, dachte, kam, las, half, wusch, machte, sah, fuhr, trank.

Activity 4
„Was <u>hast</u> du am Wochenende <u>gemacht</u>?"
„Leider nichts Interessantes. Ich <u>habe</u> <u>geputzt</u>."
„Ach nein. Warum denn?"
„Meine Mutter <u>hat</u> mich <u>besucht</u>. Sie <u>hat</u> einen guten Kuchen <u>mitgebracht</u>, aber sonst war es schrecklich. Sie <u>hat</u> die ganze Zeit <u>gefragt</u>, 'Warum <u>hast</u> du das dort <u>gestellt</u>? Warum hast du noch nicht <u>tapeziert</u>? Warum hast du dir solche komischen Möbel <u>gekauft</u>. . .?'"
„Und was <u>hast</u> du dazu <u>gesagt</u>?"
„'Ich <u>habe</u> sehr wenig Zeit <u>gehabt</u>. In den letzten Wochen <u>habe</u> ich sehr viel <u>gelernt</u> und <u>(habe)</u> mich überhaupt nicht für Hausarbeit <u>interessiert</u>.' Dann <u>hat</u> sie mir ein Kochbuch <u>gegeben</u>."
„Und du <u>hast</u> dich bestimmt <u>aufgeregt</u>!"

Activity 5
1. intransitive 2. transitive 3. intransitive 4. transitive
5. transitive 6. intransitive.

Activity 6
Grüsse aus Griechenland!
Gestern <u>haben</u> wir diese Insel <u>besucht</u>. Wir <u>sind</u> zwei Stunden mit dem Boot <u>gefahren</u>, dann <u>sind</u> wir auf einen Berg <u>gestiegen</u>. Wir <u>haben</u> die Aussicht <u>bewundert</u> und <u>sind</u> <u>eingeschlafen</u>! Später <u>sind</u> wir im Meer <u>geschwommen</u> und <u>haben</u> in der Sonne <u>gesessen</u>. Die Zeit <u>ist</u> sehr schnell <u>vergangen</u> . . . Leider <u>habe</u> ich eine sehr rote Nase <u>bekommen</u>.
Alles Gute
Helmut und Klara

Activity 7
1. Sie wird spät nach Hause kommen.
2. Du wirst einen Sonnenbrand bekommen!
3. Wir werden ins Kino gehen.
4. Ich werde Suppe kochen.
5. Ihr werdet zuviel Lärm machen.

Activity 8

1. Wenn ich durstig bin, trinke ich eine Tasse Tee.
   Wenn ich durstig bin, werde ich eine Tasse Tee trinken.
   Wenn ich durstig wäre, würde ich eine Tasse Tee trinken/
   tränke ich eine Tasse Tee.
   Wenn ich durstig gewesen wäre, hätte ich eine Tasse Tee
   getrunken.
2. Wenn sie Hunger hat, ißt sie ein Käsebrot.
   Wenn sie Hunger hat, wird sie ein Käsebrot essen.
   Wenn sie Hunger hätte, würde sie ein Käsebrot essen/äße
   sie ein Käsebrot.
   Wenn sie Hunger gehabt hätte, hätte sie ein Käsebrot
   gegessen.
3. Wenn wir uns langweilen, sehen wir fern.
   Wenn wir uns langweilen, werden wir fernsehen.
   Wenn wir uns langweilten, würden wir fernsehen/
   sähen wir fern.
   Wenn wir uns gelangweilt hätten, hätten wir ferngesehen.
4. Wenn es regnet, bleiben die Kinder zu Hause.
   Wenn es regnet, werden die Kinder zu Hause bleiben.
   Wenn es regnete, würden die Kinder zu Hause bleiben/
   blieben die Kinder zu Hause.
   Wenn es geregnet hätte, wären die Kinder zu Hause
   geblieben.

Activity 9

Er sagte, die Theaterkarten seien zu teuer gewesen.
Sie fragte, ob er also keine gekauft habe.
Er antwortete/sagte, er habe nicht genug Geld dabeigehabt.
Sie fragte, warum er sie nicht angerufen habe.
Er sagte/antwortete, er habe ihre Telefonnummer verloren.

Activity 10

Darf, muß, wird/dürfte, wollen, kann/mag, soll, müssen,
kann/mag, muß, mag, soll, können, wollen.

Activity 11

Heute war ein katastrophaler Tag! Ich <u>hatte</u> das Haus schon <u>verlassen,</u> dann <u>ist</u> mir <u>eingefallen,</u> daß ich den Mantel nicht <u>angezogen</u> hatte. Der Bus <u>ist</u> fast ohne mich <u>abgefahren,</u> aber ich <u>bin</u> im letzten Augenblick <u>eingestiegen.</u> Dann <u>habe</u> ich <u>bemerkt,</u> daß ich mir das Hemd <u>zerrissen</u> hatte. Ich <u>habe</u> mich <u>zurückgehalten,</u> sofort auszusteigen; ich <u>bin</u> <u>weitergefahren,</u> weil ich mit einem Kollegen <u>ausgemacht</u> hatte, daß wir gemeinsam frühstücken würden. Es <u>ist</u> mir aber <u>mißlungen,</u> ohne Schaden anzukommen: ich <u>hatte</u> meine Tasche <u>vollgestopft</u> und <u>habe/hatte</u> sie dadurch <u>kaputtgemacht.</u> Bücher, Papiere, Taschentücher . . . alles <u>ist</u> beim Aussteigen <u>hinausgefallen!</u>

Activity 12

Unsere alte Nachbarin <u>wurde</u> von einem Jungen <u>angegriffen.</u> Die Polizei kam und er <u>wurde</u> <u>weggeschleppt.</u> Ihre Handtasche <u>wurde</u> von ihm <u>gegriffen</u> und sie <u>wurde</u> ins Gesicht <u>geschlagen.</u> Sie schrie sehr laut, aber ich glaube nicht, daß sie schwer <u>verletzt</u> wurde. Sie <u>wurde</u> von meiner Frau <u>beruhigt.</u> Der Verbrecher <u>wurde</u> von meinem Sohn <u>festgehalten.</u> Er ist erst 15, aber sehr kräftig! Dann <u>wurde</u> die Polizei von mir <u>angerufen</u> und dem Jungen <u>wurden</u> Handschellen <u>angelegt.</u> Entsetzlich, daß so etwas am hellen Tag <u>versucht</u> <u>wird!</u>

Activity 13

1. Ist es dir gelungen, das Restaurant zu finden?
2. Ja – und das Essen hat mir sehr gut geschmeckt.
3. Es war ein langer Weg, aber es hat sich gelohnt.
4. Es geht um eine arme deutsche Familie.
5. Es fehlt mir der Mut, das zu tun.
6. In diesem Fall wird mir das nicht gefallen.
7. Ist es dir kalt? Du kannst meinen Pullover ausleihen.
8. Es macht mir nichts aus, welchen Film wir sehen.

Activity 14

1. Steh auf – es ist schon nach acht!
2. Seid nicht so dumm!
3. Geben Sie mir bitte ein Formular!
4. Beeilt euch, sonst kommen wir zu spät!
5. Kommen Sie bitte mit!
6. Lies mir das vor!

Activity 15
1. Das Schwimmen ist sehr gesund.
2. Sie geht gern ins Theater.
3. Hast du das Kind gesehen, das in der Ecke geschlafen hat?
4. Er sitzt in der Küche und ißt Suppe.
5. Kennst du den Gitarre spielenden Mann?/Kennst du den Mann, der Gitarre spielt?/Kennst du den Gitarrenspieler?

Activity 16
1. Wir wohnen seit vier Jahren in Manchester.
2. Seit wann arbeitest du in London?
3. Er wartete seit einer Stunde, als das Telefon endlich klingelte.
4. Ich habe Tennis seit Jahren nicht (mehr) gespielt.
5. Ich wollte diesen Film seit langem sehen.
6. Seit wann kannten sie sich?

▼ Word order

Activity 1
1. Fahren Sie jeden Sommer mit Ihrer Familie nach Spanien?
2. Wenn das Wetter schön ist, können wir im Garten essen./Wir können im Garten essen, wenn das Wetter schön ist.
3. Am Samstag möchte ich einkaufen gehen./Ich möchte am Samstag einkaufen gehen.
4. Er hat gerade die gleiche Frage gestellt.
5. Ich will nicht allein gehen.
6. Ich wollte nicht den schwarzen Pulli, sondern den blauen./Den schwarzen Pulli wollte ich nicht, sondern den blauen.

Activity 2
1. Anna war am Tisch so still, **obwohl** sie sonst sehr gesprächig war.
2. Ihre Mutter wußte sofort, **daß** etwas mit ihr los war.
3. Sie wartete, **bis** sie mit dem Essen fertig war.
4. Sie sprach mit ihr, **als** sie den Tisch zusammen abräumten.
5. Sie erfuhr, **warum** sie so wenig gesagt hatte.
6. Anna hatte Angst, **weil** mehrere ihrer Arbeitskollegen entlassen worden waren.
7. Sie fragte sich, **ob** ihre Stellung sicher wäre.
8. Ihre Mutter beruhigte sie, **trotzdem** machte sie sich Sorgen um ihre Tochter.

▼ Numbers and times

Activity 1

1. zweiundzwanzig
2. dreiunddreißig
3. vierundvierzig
4. fünfundfünfzig
5. sechsundsechzig
6. siebenundsiebzig
7. achtundachtzig
8. neunundneunzig
9. dreiundzwanzig
10. zweiunddreißig

Activity 2

1. dreihundertfünfundvierzig
2. fünfhundertachtundsiebzig
3. neunhundertneunundneunzig
4. sechshundertsechsundsechzig
5. siebenhunderteinundzwanzig

Activity 3

1. zwei Uhr zehn
   zehn nach zwei
   zehn Minuten nach zwei
2. vier Uhr zwanzig
   zwanzig nach vier
   zwanzig Minuten nach vier
3. sechs Uhr fünfzig
   zehn vor sieben
   zehn Minuten vor sieben
4. acht Uhr zwölf
   zwölf nach acht
   zwölf Minuten nach acht
5. neun Uhr sechsunddreißig
   vierundzwanzig Minuten vor zehn
   sechs nach halb zehn

Activity 4

1. 10.30
2. 6.15
3. 5.30
4. 4.45
5. 6.15
6. 12.26
7. 3.33

INDEX

▼▼▼ INDEX